THE
URBANIZATION PROCESS
IN
THE THIRD WORLD

THE
URBANIZATION PROCESS
IN
THE THIRD WORLD

EXPLORATIONS IN SEARCH OF A THEORY

☆

T. G. McGEE, M.A. Ph.D.

Senior Lecturer in Geography
University of Hong Kong

LONDON: G. BELL AND SONS, LTD.

ISBN 0 7135 1623 2

Printed in Great Britain by
The Camelot Press Ltd., London and Southampton

Contents

Tables

Figures

Preface

THIS VOLUME of essays represents a selection of papers I have written since 1962. The theme of the essays in the first section is my growing disillusionment with the application of the theories that have emerged from the study of the urbanization process in the West. In 1960 when I left New Zealand for Malaya, the 'underdeveloped world' meant a 'developing world' to me. Perhaps my views were more liberal than others for I anticipated that 'development' within different political and economic systems in the underdeveloped countries would mean a progression towards the same high per-capita income enjoyed by societies of the developed world. I presumed the path of progress, allowing for slight variations within the under-developed countries, to be substantially the same as that operating in the developed countries. This 'similar path' theory contends that theoretical models utilized to explain social, economic and political changes in the Western World can be superimposed upon the Third World.

My experience in Malaya and more recently in Hong Kong has convinced me that I cannot accept the 'similar path' models when they pertain to the urbanization process in the Third World and my criticisms are set forth in my first three essays.

The second section of essays indicates how my field experience in Southeast Asia, and particularly Malaya, has reinforced my belief that the 'similar path' models are inadequate.

Two terms—the Third World and the urbanization process— require definition. *The Third World* describes that group of nations frequently labelled 'underdeveloped' which contains almost two-thirds of the world's population. Geographically it includes virtually all the countries of Africa, the Middle East,

9

Asia, and Latin America and omits 'developed' nations such as South Africa, Israel, and Japan. I have excluded the Communist countries of China, North Vietnam, North Korea and Cuba for their problems of development are being tackled in a different manner from that occurring in the non-Communist Third World nations. I believe the term 'Third World' avoids the emotional overtones of others, such as 'developing world' or 'neo-colonial world'. A politically neutral term, the 'Third World' still distinguishes its countries from those of the capitalist developed world or the Communist world.

The Urbanization Process is a concept which has many interpretations—a balloon into which each social scientist blows his own meaning. Lampard's definition of urbanization—'a way of ordering a population to attain a certain level of subsistence and security in a given environment'—is broad but contains the central conceptual meaning. Whatever the debates on the meaning, there is general agreement on the measure of the process' end product—the urbanization level—which is generally defined as the proportion of the country's total population (or designated statistical unit) resident in urban places. Hence much depends on the definition of 'urban place', and there is no general agreement on this question. However, many government authorities are moving towards defining urban concentrations based on the residence of 100,000 or more people. While 'urban place' remains a contentious term, it is accepted that an increasing urbanization level is symptomatic of a successful urbanization process.

The author wishes to gratefully acknowledge permission to reproduce the following articles: the Editors of *Pacific Viewpoint*, 'The Rural-Urban Continuum Debate. The Preindustrial City and Rural-Urban Migration', Vol. 5, No. 2, September, 1964; the Editor of *Civilisations*, 'Revolutionary Change and the Third World City: A Theory of Urban Involution', Vol. XVIII, No. 3, 1968; the New Zealand Geographical Society, 'An Aspect of Urbanisation in Southeast Asia. The Process of Cityward Migration'. *Proceedings Fourth New Zealand Geography Conference*, 1965, and the Editor, *The Journal of Tropical Geography*, 'The Cultural Role of Cities: A Case Study of Kuala Lumpur', Vol. 17, May 1963.

PART ONE

THEORETICAL EXPLORATIONS

The Urbanization Process:
Western Theory & Third World Reality

INTRODUCTION

TWO VISIONS haunt the intellectuals who view the urbanization process in the Third World.[1] In the first vision the cities are seen as 'enclaves' surrounded by a hostile peasantry. In these enclaves foppish elites play luxurious games with the power and wealth they have inherited or created since Independence. In the other vision the cities are seen as 'beach-heads', centres of modernization which act as the catalysts for economic growth, the centres from which the benefits of modernization flow outwards to revitalize the stagnating agricultural sector.

It would be foolish to deny that these visions have ideological overtones. Indeed the language of description, 'beach-head' and 'enclave', reflects the military terms of battle. In an era when Vietnam has come increasingly to prod the conscience of the intellectual, this is hardly surprising. The ideological overtones are there: in the eyes of Fanon, Frank or Lin Piao, the cities of the Third World are capitalist structures decaying because of the inevitable decay of capitalism itself.[2] From exactly the opposite point of view, writers such as Hirschman or Friedmann see the strength of these countries lying primarily in their cities because as capitalist structures they have the capacity for economic growth which has characterized the developed capitalist nations, most notably the United States.[3]

In my view both sides overstate their case because their assumptions ignore the reality of the Third World urbanization process. In this essay I have attempted to evaluate some of the most prevalent theoretical assumptions concerning the urbanization process in the Third World.

On one issue there is little debate—the cities of the Third World are growing rapidly. The statistics of this growth have been plotted in a large number of publications and need not be recounted in great detail here.[4] What needs emphasis is the fact that the growth of the urban population in the underdeveloped world appears to be occurring at a much faster rate than the growth of urban population in their comparable period of European growth.

As Kingsley Davis has pointed out:

> In 34 underdeveloped countries for which we have data relating to the 1940's and 1950's, the average annual gain in the urban population was 4·5 per cent. The figure is remarkably similar for the various regions: 4·7 per cent in seven countries of Africa, 4·7 per cent in 15 countries in Asia and 4·3 per cent in 12 countries of Latin America. In contrast, in nine European countries during their period of fastest urban population growth (mostly in the latter half of the 19th Century) the average gain per year was 2·1 per cent.[5]

It is true that there are marked regional variations in the level and rates of urbanization. For instance it has been recently suggested that 'more than half the people of most Latin-American countries are no longer rural, and a fifth to a third live in cities of 100,000 or more'.[6] This contrasts with the continent of Africa with 13 per cent of its population living in urban areas and South Asia with 14 per cent. Of course there are exceptions—some individual countries have much higher levels of urbanization within these broad realms. In Asia, Malaysia and Taiwan have at least 40 per cent of their population living in urban areas. In the Middle East, Israel, the United Arab Republic and Lebanon are already well urbanized.

But throughout the Third World the population are still largely rural dwellers. Urban growth still continues, however, at an accelerating rate of up to 8 per cent annually. As one authority points out, this means cities 'are doubling their populations every ten to fifteen years'.[7]

This dramatic growth would seem to suggest that the

countries of the Third World are passing through an 'urban revolution' similar to that which characterized the countries of the developed world, that eventually they will become urban nations with perhaps 70 to 80 per cent of their population living in urban areas; that eventually these countries will form part of what Toynbee has called the 'World City'.[8] If this is so, the theories which have been developed out of the Western experience must be acceptable in interpreting and predicting the pattern of urbanization in the Third World.

CITY TO THE FORE: Unravelling the Urbanization Process

Customarily the urbanization process in the underdeveloped world is regarded as identical to that which occurred in the Western industrial nations of the capitalist world. Reissman states:

All this is by way of introduction to a dominating theme of this book: that industrial urban development in the West and in the underdeveloped countries today is the same process although greatly separated in time and place.[9]

While Reissman does admit certain differences in the framework of conditions within which the urbanization process is occurring in the underdeveloped world, he still interprets this urbanization process as being repetitive of the Western experience: 'it is our assumption that the history of the West from the nineteenth century onward is being reiterated in the underdeveloped countries today.'[10]

The inference of this assumption is clear enough. If the urbanization process in the underdeveloped world is the same as that which occurred in the West, then it is possible to suggest that some kind of theoretical model focusing on Western experience can be utilized in the interpretation of the urbanization process in the Third World.

Broadly speaking, it is possible to delineate three main facets of the urbanization process. The first is demographic; the second, economic; and the third, social.[11]

The demographic aspects of the urbanization process were twofold: (i) cities grew rapidly in the developing capitalist world from 1800 onwards, and (ii) the total proportion of population resident in cities increased compared to that resident in rural areas. It is wise to keep these two parts of the demographic process of urbanization separated for analytical purposes, as will be seen in a later section. Henceforth, the term 'urban growth' will mean the same as 'city growth'. The term 'urbanization level' will mean simply the proportion of a country's total population 'resident in urban areas'.

The demographic features of the 'urban revolution' in the developed capitalist countries have been traced by several writers.[12] Typically, the cycle of urbanization in these developed countries tends to be represented by a curve in the shape of an attenuated S. Davis describes it:

> Starting from the bottom of the S, the first bend tends to come early and to be followed by a long attenuation. In the United Kingdom, for instance, the swiftest rise in the proportion of people living in the cities of 100,000 or larger occurred from 1811 to 1851. In the U.S. it occurred from 1820 to 1890, in Greece from 1879 to 1921. As the proportion climbs above 50 per cent the curve begins to flatten out; it falters, or even declines, when the proportion urban has reached about 75 per cent. In the United Kingdom, one of the world's most urban countries, the proportion was slightly higher in 1926 (78·7 per cent) than in 1961 (78·3 per cent).[13]

Davis describes the demographic components of this increase in cities leading to urbanization in the industrialized nations. Cities grow in three ways: (i) because of population growth, settlements previously classified as rural are re-classified as urban; (ii) through an excess of births over deaths (natural increase); and (iii) because people have moved from the non-urban to the urban areas. Davis indicates that the first component of urban increase was of little significance to the history of the growth of cities in the industrialized nations. The second factor was of scarcely more significance for mortality in the cities was much higher than in the rural areas and the birth rates were lower. Therefore, the shift of population from rural to urban areas becomes the principal component of population growth in the cities. This indeed appears to have been the case in the urbanization of the majority of the developed and industrialized, capitalist countries.

To understand why this rural–urban migration occurred, one must evaluate the economic facets of the urbanization process. The principal economic feature of the process was the shift from agricultural to non-agricultural occupations. Once again, the historical experience of the industrialized Western World was that this process, while it occurred at varying rates from country to country, was the basis of their increase in the levels of economic productivity. Davis has explained the reasons for this structural shift in employment as follows:

> The reason was that the rise in technological enhancement of human productivity, together with certain constant factors, rewarded urban concentration. One of the constant factors was that agriculture uses land as its prime instrument of production and hence spreads out people who are engaged in it, whereas manufacturing, commerce and services use land only as a site. Moreover, the demand for agricultural products is less elastic than the demand for services and manufactures. As productivity grows, services and manufactures can absorb more manpower by paying higher wages. Since non-agricultural activities can use land simply as a site, they can locate near one another (in towns and cities) and thus minimize the friction of space inevitably involved in the division of labor. At the same time, as agricultural technology is improved, capital costs in farming rise and manpower becomes not only less needed but also economically more burdensome. A substantial portion of the agricultural population is therefore sufficiently disadvantaged, in relative terms, to be attracted by higher wages in other sectors.[14]

The sum total of this economic revolution, often more popularly labelled 'The Industrial Revolution',[15] was the basis of the rise in the levels of these societies' economic development. Hence, urbanization has come to be understood in the Western World in terms of its 'connection with economic growth',[16] generally being associated with the level of a nation's economic development. The relevance of this inferred association and, in particular, the role that cities play in the process of economic development will be discussed in the section on the theories which have grown out of the empirical circumstances of the Western urbanization process.

Finally, the urbanization process in the developed industrial countries, it is argued, was responsible for radical social change. Reissman's words sum up the views of many Western social scientists:

> Urbanization is social change on a vast scale. It means deep and irrevocable changes that alter all sectors of a society. . . . Apparently the process is irreversible once begun. The impetus of urbanization upon society is such that society gives way to urban institutions, urban value, and urban demands.[17]

There is no area of human existence which is not influenced—the family becomes smaller, religion loses its important position, new social structures emerge, new 'power' and 'class' patterns characterize the social structure and behaviour patterns are changed. Urban society as a distinct entity emerges.

This brief résumé of the principal features of the urban process in the industrialized nations of the West now needs to be looked at in terms of the theories which have evolved out of this investigation and which have come to dominate social science models in the Anglo-Saxon world. The significance which the theorists attach to the influence of the city emerges strikingly. Benet's comment on the role of the city in urban sociology sums up these approaches. 'The city was the key variable, a social subsystem which came to be all-inclusive.'[18] It will become clear from my analysis that by putting the emphasis on the 'subsystem', if in fact we can use this term interchangeably with 'settlement unit', and by ignoring the total system, these theorists have been side-tracked. For, as I shall argue later, cities are simply a reflection of a wider socio-economic system, and within the context of the underdeveloped world, each country has been shaped and moulded by the penetration of other socio-economic systems. To make my position quite clear, I believe that, by postulating the city as the independent variable, the theorists are guilty of saying that the symptom has caused the disease and that is highly improbable.

First, let us consider the demographic theory which grew out of the investigation of the urbanization process in the developed world. This theory has been labelled 'the demographic transition'. Following Petersen[19] three main population types may be designated. The first, the 'preindustrial type' characterized by high birth rates, high crude death and infant mortality rates, led to a relatively stable, young and small population. Industrialization and urbanization introduced a second phase labelled by Petersen the 'early Western population type' when because mortality was reduced and the birth rate remained high, the population increased rapidly. As Petersen writes:

> The early Western population type is characterized by a gradual conquest of hunger and disease, while the norms favoring large families still remain more or less unchanged. Population growth, therefore is rapid.[20]

This phase of population growth (associated with rapid urbanization, industrialization and a changing social structure) led to a third population type, the 'Modern Western Society', characterized by relatively low birth rates, very low infant mortality rates and low mortality rates, leading to a relatively stable, older and larger population.

At the moment it is unnecessary to consider the fact that historical demography has rendered many features of this theory suspect,[21] but it is important to consider what variables are said to be influencing the process of demographic transition. The two most important independent variables are (i) technologies of birth and death control, and (ii) the socio-cultural system of the society or societies undergoing transition. The important point here is that while the mortality patterns are directly affected by death control, the adoption of birth control techniques is greatly affected by the values of the emerging middle classes. Thus we find that fertility declines first within the newly emerging professional and managerial classes concentrated in the cities.[22] Over a period of time, fertility gradually declines throughout the various class groups. Because the fertility patterns tend to be associated with social and behavioural changes thought to be induced by urbanization, the city is central to the theory of the demographic transition. Petersen's summary of the changes affecting population growth illustrates this point.

One of the important ways that industrialization affected Western population growth was to shift so large a proportion of the village-born people to the towns that the way of life of the urban middle class eventually became the norm of all. Rational death control was followed, after a considerable interim, by rational birth control.[23]

Thus rational birth control became part of the urban, middle class way-of-life. In the next section we shall consider what relevance this theory has to the investigation of the Third World.

A second group of theories concerned with putting forward a model of economic growth was based upon the analysis of the urbanization process in the West. For these theorists the history of economic growth in the developed, capitalist world had shown economic development to be associated with two broad processes: (i) A structural change in occupations occurred whereby the agricultural labour force shifted to manufacturing concurrent with the Industrial Revolution. With continuing economic development, this phase led to a majority of the population being engaged in service or tertiary occupations; and (ii) a process of urbanization occurred when the population shifted from the rural to the urban sector. It was natural, therefore, that the economic growth analysis in the developed countries should associate economic development with urbanization. One finds this assumption in virtually all writings concerning economic growth. For instance, Sjoberg says: 'Economic development, it seems clear, demands expansion of the urban sector',[24] Berry echoes Sjoberg when he claims 'that economic advancement is related to urbanization, and that increasing specialization and continued urban growth go hand in hand'.[25] The rationale for these assertions is well expressed by Lampard.

Specialization of functions makes inevitably for specialization of areas: it promotes a territorial division of labor between town and country and differentiates town from town. . . . The closer integration of interdependent functions means that less of a community's limited stock of energy and material need to be devoted to overcoming the various disutilities thus an ecological response to certain tech-

20

nological and cost considerations which impel a more selective use of space . . . city growth is simply the concentration of differentiated but functionally—integrated specialisms in rational locales. The modern city is a mode of social organization which furthers efficiency in economic activity.[26]

At this stage, there is no need to take issue with this argument that the city is a result of a need for efficiency in economic activity, but one might argue whether the supposed efficiency in economic activity outweighs the social and political problems which frequently accompany this increased economic efficiency. This theory of economic development, based on the empirical investigation of the Western countries' experience clearly argues that a locational revolution accompanies the economic revolution, thereby stressing the importance of city growth. The theoretical advantages of this model to overall economic growth have been expressed by the economist Hirschman[27] who favours heavy investment in the capital-intensive sectors at early stages of economic growth with the full understanding that such a policy may be responsible for imbalances (both regional and structural). Ultimately, however, it will lead to overall growth and a trickling down of wealth to the slow-growing areas. Whether such an economic programme would indeed bring about this situation does not matter for the moment. In broad terms, it focuses investment on the leading sector (most obviously the urban sector) and presumably causes city growth. Another example of this viewpoint of the urbanization process can be found in Rostow's[28] *The Stages of Economic Growth* which assumes an 'urban revolution' of the same dimensions as that which occurred in the developed societies for the underdeveloped world, based on a historical model of economic growth. In the next section we shall consider the validity of this and other economic models.

The final group of theories growing out of the investigation of Western urbanization are those theories concerned with the supposed positive role of the city in inducing social change. Broadly, the theories that developed here can be treated in three sections. (i) Some considered the city to be the centre of social change, introducing new social patterns and breaking down the old, traditional pattern; (ii) Some argued that new social patterns in the city had begun to spread outwards to the rural areas. Hence, in a social sense, urbanization was not limited purely to the boundaries of a city or to any area defined as 'urban'; and (iii) Some argued that the cities, as significant social subsystems, caused specific features of personal behaviour in a person residing therein. Basic to all these theories was the assumption that there were distinct rural–urban differences which were measurable and quantifiable. These ideas of rural–urban distinctions have been built into a broad model of social theory which has come to dominate a large amount of thinking in Western sociology. We may label this group of theorists the 'rural–urban continuum' thinkers.

Since the growth of these theories is discussed in a later paper in this volume,[29] I shall not discuss them in any great detail here. Suffice to say that this group of theorists suggested that certain demographic conditions which were thought to characterize town life; that large size of population, high densities of population and heterogeneous populations could induce changes in the personality and social life of the town dweller which would not occur in the country dweller. It was a short step from these arguments to see the city as a crucible of cultural and social change. Thus the environment of the city is seen as the crucial variable in any theory of social change.

CRITICISMS OF THE 'CITY-DOMINANT' THEORIES

The previous section has outlined the major city-dominant theories based on Western experience. Many writers have argued that the underdeveloped world is undergoing a repetitive process of urbanization. This section evaluates the adequacy of this assumption when applied to the underdeveloped world.

First let us consider the adequacy of the *theory of demographic transition*, and in particular, its relevance to supposed rural–urban differentials that exist in the demographic characteristics of the population. Most writers now agree that the theory of the demographic transition as it was developed on the basis of the Western experience is not only inadequate for the context of the underdeveloped world, but is scarcely adequate in explaining the patterns of fertility increase experienced in the post-war 'baby boom' in the developed countries. The most trenchant criticisms of the demographic transition on the basis of the investigation of the demographic patterns has been carried out by Janet Abu-Lughod.[30] In the course of applying certain broadly-accepted generalizations concerning rural–urban demographic differentials which had grown out of the Western experience to the case of Egypt, she found that Egypt evinced startling differentials. For instance, the Western experience has generally argued that urban fertility is lower than rural fertility. Evidence in the Egyptian case indicates that urban and rural fertility patterns are substantially the same, and this situation has existed for some considerable time. Secondly, the Western experience indicated that rural death rates were generally lower than urban death rates during the early phases of urbanization. The investigation of the Egyptian case, Abu-Lughod points out, indicates almost exactly the opposite. Urban mortality rates are substantially below those of rural areas. Thirdly, as a corollary of these earlier generalizations, it can be argued that because the birth rates are high in urban areas and death rates lower, at least compared to the Western experience, then urban population growth from natural increase is considerably higher than the rural population increase. The Egyptian study indicates that, population increase in Cairo, the largest urban area, is now growing substantially from natural increase at a rate almost one-third higher than that of the rural areas. The relevance of this particular fact to the process of urbanization is of extreme significance.

The other generalizations based on the Western experience—namely, the likely demographic composition of populations, the sex ratio and marital status—need not concern us immediately, for it is the variants in the dynamics of population growth between this underdeveloped country and the developed countries at 'similar phases' of economic growth and urbanization which have relevance to any model of urbanization in this and other underdeveloped countries. Abu-Lughod in attempting to explain the variances between Egypt and the Western world suggests that they can be explained primarily by two factors: (a) technologies of birth and death control which exist

23

at a particular stage of the demographic 'take-off'; and (*b*) the socio-cultural system of the society which is undergoing the transition. If these two variables are accepted, then it is possible to postulate a theory of the demographic transition which takes into account the time at which a country is embarked upon the process of demographic take-off. Thus, for instance, the rural-urban differentials in mortality decline said to characterize the Western European experience cannot be applied to many of the Third World countries today where the technology of death control is so much more advanced and effective; and spatially can be said to be generally penetrating from urban to rural. The generalization with respect to the birth control is rather more difficult to establish. The technologies of birth control are more advanced in the contemporary world than they were during the early phases of industrialization. The use of birth control depends upon its acceptance, and as yet the evidence for widespread acceptance of birth control, particularly in the 'heavily-populated' countries of the underdeveloped world, is not widespread.

It is clear that the points which Abu-Lughod makes about the differentials in fertility, mortality and natural increase at the different times of population take-off are valid, but, of course, their application varies considerably from country to country in the underdeveloped world. Its generality is particularly suspect in societies where one finds substantial ethnic differences which have spatial ramifications. Malaya, for instance, represents just such a society. In a society where urban–rural differentials really have in the past presented nothing more than non-Malay/Malay differentials, the generality of such arguments must be evaluated extremely carefully. This does not mean, however, that the relevance of the general argument to the process of urbanization is lost.

For if the contributions of the relative components of population growth in these cities are different from that which occurred in the growth of cities in the Western World, then there is good reason to believe that the process of urbanization and the process of population redistribution will also be different. Abu-Lughod is well aware of this fact when she suggests that in certain of the overpopulated, under-industrialized countries, such as India, it may well be that the rates of natural increase are so high in the cities that the process of urbanization (i.e. the shift in population from rural to urban area) is not occurring at the same rates as in the developed world. Cities grow, certainly, but they grow from natural increase just as much as from rural–urban migration, as opposed to the rather different circumstances in Western Europe and the United States. Davis has enlarged upon this argument[31] and I have argued that the process of urbanization might be more accurately labelled 'pseudo-urbanization'.[32] In some Third World countries, then, city growth is not to be equated with urbanization, and thus one may argue that the redistribution of population from the rural areas to the urban (said to be so basic to the process of economic growth) is not occurring and raises the whole question (dealt with in the next section) as to what implications this has to the possibilities of economic growth and the inevitability of the urban revolution.

An evaluation of the economic theories which rely upon the Western experience for models of the form of economic growth which either will or will not occur in the under-developed world follows. One of the best criticisms of the prominent Anglo-Saxon theories of economic growth has been put forth by André Gundar Frank.[33] In an exhaustive review of what he labels the 'sociology of development' as it has emerged primarily in the United States, he indicates the grave in-adequacy of many of these theories particularly with respect to the underdeveloped world. From the point of this argument, there is no need to repeat his review or criticism at great length. Frank's review of these theories clearly shows how much they rely on the city's being the leading sector of economic growth and a crucible of social change. Thus Hoselitz argues that underdeveloped countries characterized by pattern variables (particularism, etc.) which hinder economic development must change to universalism and achievement orientation for economic development to occur. Such changes, it is argued, clearly will be city-focused.[34] This is also shown in his discussion of the association of 'rationalization'; its association with urbanization; and its role in the growth of the market economy[35].

A second group of theorists arguing that economic progress in the underdeveloped world will occur primarily because of the diffusion from the West of capital, institutions and technology through the Third World city draws Frank's acid criticism. He shows the way in which private foreign capital and technology tend to concentrate in the capital-intensive sectors, often of the metropolis, preventing the entry of domestic capital. The diffusionists place great emphasis on *social mobility* and the growth of the middle class.[36] As Frank points out, this social mobility is primarily *individual* mobility and does not transform social structures 'rather, a change in the social structure may render possible social mobility and economic development'.[37] Indeed, there is considerable evidence to suggest in the underdeveloped world that the growth of the middle class renders the distribution of income not more but *less* equal. Thus the growth of the middle class (a city-based phenomenon) does not necessarily mean economic growth.

Finally, Frank also considers the behaviouralists (represented by Hagen[38] and McClelland[39]) who stress the role of individual motivation and the need for achievement to bring about economic development and cultural change. This approach moves away from the social environment to the *individual personality* and presumably relies much less on the assumptions of city or rural environment as being basic to the creation of economic development.

Central to Frank's criticism is that these theories, which in varying degrees all expect the Western experience to be repeated, are totally incorrect, for the condition of under-development in the Third World has been generated by the impact of capitalism and can only be understood through its continuing relationship with that system. Thus the 'Sociologists of development', in Frank's words, suffer from a fatal 'sociological dualism'.

Their whole theory and theorizing is split down the middle. They see one set of characteristics, take note of one social structure, if any; construct one theory for one part of the [*sic*] what has been one world economic and social system for half a millennium, and construct another pattern and theory for the other part.[40]

The implications of Frank's 'holistic' theory to the analysis of the structural characteristics of the underdeveloped world's cities—the roles they play in economic development and, indeed, all economic facets of the urbanization process—cannot be overemphasized. One of the most relevant implications is the question of changes in the occupational structure which are said to accompany the urbanization process. As I have already commented, one of the most enduring theories to emerge from the Western experience has been that which postulates the change from agricultural to manufacturing occupations and thence to tertiary-dominated occupations. The empirical evidence for an identical change in occupational structures of many underdeveloped countries is not strong.[41] The pattern now appears to be 'that urbanization is proceeding at a more rapid pace than the expansion of manufacturing employment, resulting in a direct shift out of agriculture into services'.[42] Thus it is the tertiary sector that is growing most obviously in the capital cities of the Third World. In itself, this does not mean that economic development or that the locational shift in population from rural to urban is not occurring, because these tertiary services are primarily urban-located. But when this factor is associated with the evidence of 'pseudo-urbanization' outlined earlier and the slow rates of increased industrial employment, then it may be argued that a very different occupational pattern exists. The reasons for this tertiarization of the Third World cities are many. In some countries where industrial production has increased, it has not meant an increase in industrial employment for it resulted largely from capital-intensive industrialization, not labour-intensive. In areas where industrialization has not increased greatly, tertiarization seems to present a dangerous sign for economic growth because of its association with growing under-employment and unemployment.

Not surprisingly there is much argument over this last assertion for some writers have argued that these poor dwellers who occupy these tertiary sectors represent a revolutionary force.[43] A growing body of research (particularly focused on Latin America) claims there is little justification for this claim.[44] In a later paper in this volume the same conclusion is arrived at but for different reasons. In this paper it is argued that the dualistic economic structure of the Third World city and its relationship with the rural hinterland will prevent the emergence of such a revolutionary demand among the urban poor in the short term.[45]

Finally, the theory of social change formulated by the city-dominant theory needs to be critically evaluated. Various researchers[46] have found that the rural-urban theory of social change inadequate for the supposedly independent variable of the city environment could not be proven as the main determinant of social change.

Rather it seems that some structural framework (which ignores the rural–urban distinction) based on some model of the prevailing systems of production might prove more adequate. Thus following Franklin's[47] threefold division of peasant, capitalist, and socialist systems of production in which 'the fundamental differentiator is the labour commitment of the enterprise',[48] a conceptual framework is provided which can be used for analytical purposes. The peasant economy is characterized by the commitment of the *chef d'enterprise* to the utilization of his family (kin). The capitalist and socialist systems of production exist because 'labour becomes a commodity to be hired and dismissed by the enterprise'.[49] This is a scheme, as Franklin has pointed out, which is not impinged upon by the agricultural-industrial division or the rural–urban division.

Working within one system of production does not automatically mean that the individual's social relationships will be of a particular type; nor does it mean that his position in the social structure will be predetermined. The point is that the mix or degree of prevalence of these two systems within a city will govern the overall social structure.

A structural framework based on the prevailing systems of economic production is, of course, only a beginning—an analytical framework of a necessarily static character. To give it more meaning, a dynamic quality must be built into the model. Since the majority of the underdeveloped nations are basically peasant systems being actively penetrated by capitalism,[50] a dynamic model can be created. This process of capitalist penetration into the peasant system does not always involve the collapse of the peasant system of production and its replacement by the capitalist system. The creation of new attitudes; a new range of felt needs—for shoes, bicycles, manufactured furniture and so on—can gradually cause the decline of uncompetitive cottage industries, or it can motivate a young peasant to move to the city to acquire these possessions. In the areas of peasant production then the capitalist penetration affects people's attitudes and changes the system itself by encouraging such features as the concentration of landownership and the creation of a rural *lumpen-proletariat*. Thus an understanding of the economic structure of the society and the economic processes which are occurring is central to the analysis of the process of urbanization.

It is therefore necessary to avoid the assertion that geographical mobility—involving the move of a population from the countryside to the city—is to be equated with social or economic mobility.[51] The physical move may introduce the individual into another mode of economic production or another set of social relations, but this does not mean an all-encompassing mobility—simply an introduction to new types of economic activity and social relations. This point, I believe, is established in my later discussion of Malay occupational mobility. (See Chapter 6.)

Many researchers would argue that the bald analysis of population movement to the cities within this economic framework is not enough. In Mitchell's[52] view, this simply identifies the 'historical' or 'processive' overall changes in the economic system. It does not explain the 'situational change' or those changes 'in behaviour following participation in different social systems'.[53] In his view, there are certain external determinants, 'some of which are characteristic of cities everywhere'.[54] His list of these determinants includes density of settlement, mobility, heterogeneity, demographic disproportion, economic differentiation, and administrative and political structures.[55] These characteristics occur in distinct sets so as to give each city a unique entity. He quotes Southall's[56] distinction between the old, established towns of British and French West Africa where research has shown that a very different social structure[57] exists compared to that in the towns whose rapid growth is based on industrial and commercial development, in the Copperbelt of Rhodesia and in South Africa. For instance, Mitchell cites Bascom's (1959) research in which the 'basic mechanisms of interaction at the personal level in Yoruba towns . . . is lineage rather than a set of specifically *urban* factors'.[58] On the other hand, Epstein's work shows clearly that in the Copperbelt towns, new patterns of social relations do come to dominate the African dwellers.

> On the towns of the Copperbelt Africans can no longer live and work together on the basis of kinship and affinity as they do in their rural villages, and many of the customs and features of the tribal system fall into desuetude.[59]

In terms of the model of economic systems, the statements that different social systems exist is predictable since the cities of West Africa have a large bazaar system (peasant system) while those of the Copperbelt are virtually capitalist-dominated.

Some writers have argued that this dualistic division between the peasant economy and capitalist economy is too simple. There is, to use Mayer's words, a 'third field of economic activity . . . ruled by its own standards which partly resemble each of the other two kinds'.[60] In this case he refers to economic activities of the 'Red-Xhosa' migrants within their urban locations. His discussion of these activities stresses the importance of personal ties and the emphasis on carrying out business with people of one's own *amakhaya* or 'home people'. He does not discuss labour commitment in sufficiently precise terms to permit analysis in terms of the original peasant economy. However, his viewpoint appears to support the concept of *situational change*.

Similarly, the case put forward by Mitchell for the analysis of social relations within a framework of the structural relationships of work or associations; the categorical relationship of race and personal networks accepts this view of *situational change*. The crux of the matter as put forward by Mayer and Mitchell is simply that the 'city situation' induces in the migrant population different patterns of economic activity and social relations from those which existed before their move to the city. This seems irrefutable. It can be labelled 'social change' or 'economic change' as a matter of course. But it cannot be inevitably labelled 'societal change' or 'economic growth'. These are structural changes occurring at a societal level.

CONCLUSION

I hope the preceding discussion has focused the reader's attention on the current of assumptions and argument which at present characterize the assessment of the urbanization in the Third World. Although the form of the urbanization process in the Third World may appear to be the same as that which characterized the West, the different *mix* of the components of the urbanization process in the Third World suggests that this factor is of such importance that at least one element of Western theory should be discarded when investigating the Third World city. This is the view that the city is an inducer of change. Benet's comment on the role of the city in Western sociological theory (already quoted) sums up these approaches—'The city was the key variable, a social sub-system which became all inclusive.'

But in the context of the majority of Third World countries, it seems that a theoretical framework which regards the city as the prime catalyst of change must be discarded. Rather, the city must be seen as a symptom of processes operating at a societal level. Thus to diagnose accurately the characteristics and roles of these cities, one must investigate the condition of underdevelopment which characterizes these countries, of which the cities are only part.

NOTES

1. Of course, to claim that there are only two visions is a gross over-simplification, for there are many viewpoints between these polar types.

2. See Frantz Fanon, *The Damned* (trs.), Constance Farington, Paris, 1963, André Gundar Frank, *Capitalism and Underdevelopment in Latin America*, New York, 1967, and Lin Piao, 'Long Live the Victory of the People's War', *Peking Review*, September 3, 1965, pp. 9–30

3. See A. O. Hirschman, *The Strategy of Economic Development*, New Haven, Connecticut, 1958, and John Friedmann, 'The Strategy of Deliberate Urbanization', *Journal of the Institute of American Planners*, XXIV, 6, November, 1968, pp. 364–73

4. For instance, see, Gerald Breese (ed.), *The City in Newly Developing Countries*, Englewood Cliffs, New Jersey, 1968

5. Kingsley Davis, 'The Urbanization of the Human Population', in Breese, ibid., p. 15

6. Joan Nelson, 'The Urban Poor Disruption or Political Integration in Third World Cities', *World Politics*, XXII, 3 April, 1970, p. 393

7. Ibid., p. 393

8. See Arnold Toynbee, 'The coming World-City' *The Times*, *Saturday Review*, July 18, 1970, p. 5

9. Leonard Reissman, *The Urban Process, Cities in Industrial Societies*, Glencoe, Illinois, 1964, pp. 167–8

10. Ibid., p. 158

11. These three facets can be equated with Lampard's division of '. . . three conceptions of urbanization in the social sciences: the behavioural, the structural and the demographic'. Eric E. Lampard, 'Historical Aspects of Urbanization', in Philip M. Hauser, and Leo F. Schnore (eds.) *The Study of Urbanization, New York*, 1965, p. 519

12. See Philip M. Hauser (ed.), *Urbanization in Asia and the Far East*, Calcutta, 1957, pp. 53 et seq.; Eric E. Lampard, ibid., pp. 519 et seq., and Davis, op. cit., pp. 5–20

13. Davis, op. cit., p. 11

14. Ibid., p. 13

15. See C. E. Ayres, *The Industrial Economy. Its Technological Basis and Institutional Destiny*. Cambridge, Mass., 1952, pp. 62–93 for one of the clearest expositions of the industrial revolution.

16. Davis, op. cit., p. 11

17. Reissman, op. cit., p. 154

18. Francisco Benet, 'Sociology Uncertain: The Ideology of the Rural-Urban Continuum', *Comparative Studies in Society and History*, VI, October, 1963, p. 3

19. See William Petersen, *Population*, New York, 1961

20. Ibid., p. 12

21. Demographers disagree on the relative contribution of deaths and births to 'natural increase' during the industrial revolution, particularly in England. See H. J. Habakkuk, 'English Population in the Eighteenth Century', *Economic History Review*, 6, 2, 1953, pp. 117–33; J. T. Krause, 'Changes in English Fertility and Mortality, 1781–1850', *Economic History Review*, 11, 1, 1958, pp. 52–70, and 'Some Implications of Recent Work in Historical Demography', *Comparative Studies in Society and History*, 1, 2, pp. 164–88

22. See Janet Abu-Lughod, 'Urban-Rural Differences as a Function of the Demographic Transition: Egyptian Data and an Analytical Model', *American Journal of Sociology*, 69, 1964, pp. 476–90

23. Petersen, op. cit., p. 12

24. Gideon Sjoberg 'Rural–Urban Balance and Models of Economic

Development', in Neil J. Smelser and Seymour M. Lipset (eds.), *Social Structure and Mobility in Economic Development*, London, 1966, p. 237

25. Brian J. L. Berry, 'Some Relations of Urbanization and Basic Patterns of Economic Development' in Forrest R. Pitts (ed.), *Urban Systems and Economic Development*, Oregon, 1962, p. 15

26. Eric E. Lampard, 'The History of Cities in the Economically Advanced Areas' in John Friedmann and William Alonso (eds.), *Regional Development and Planning*, Cambridge, Mass., 1964, p. 332

27. Hirschman, op. cit.

28. See W. W. Rostow, *The Stages of Economic Growth: A Non-Communist Manifesto*, Cambridge, 1967

29. See Chapter 2, pp. 35–63

30. Janet Abu-Lughod, op. cit., pp. 476–90

31. Davis, op. cit., p. 520

32. See T. G. McGee, *The Southeast Asian City*, London, 1967

33. See André Gundar Frank, 'Sociology of Development, and Underdevelopment of Sociology', *Catalyst*, 3, Summer 1967, pp. 20–73

34. See Bert F. Hoselitz, *The Sociological Aspects of Economic Growth*, Glencoe, Illinois

35. See Bert F. Hoselitz, 'The Market Matrix' in Wilbert E. Moore and Arnold S. Feldman (eds.), *Labor Commitment and Social Change in Developing Areas*, New York, 1960, pp. 222 et. seq.

36. As an example of this approach see Gino Germani, 'Social and Political Consequences of Mobility' in Smelser and Lipset, op. cit., 1966, pp. 364–94

37. Frank, op. cit., p. 58

38. See Everett E. Hagen, *On The Theory of Social Change*, Homewood, Illinois, 1962

39. David McClelland, *The Achieving Society*, Princeton, New Jersey, 1961

40. Frank, op. cit., p. 72

41. See S. G. Trantis, 'The Economic Progress, Occupational Distribution and International Terms of Trade', *Economic Journal*, LXIII, 1953, pp. 627–37, and W. Arthur Lewis, 'Unemployment in Developing Countries', *The World Today*, 1, January, 1967, pp. 13–22

42. Wilbert E. Moore, 'Changes in Occupational Structures' in Smelser and Lipset, op. cit., p. 203

43. See, for instance, Fanon, op. cit.

44. See Oscar Lewis, *Five Families. Mexican Case Studies in the Culture of Poverty*, New York, 1959; Nelson, op. cit., and Wayne A. Cornelius Jr., 'Urbanization as an Agent in Latin American Political Instability: The Case of Mexico', *The American Political Science Review*, 63, 3, 1969, pp. 833–57

45. See Chapter 3, pp. 64–94

46. For instance see, Oscar Lewis, 'Urbanization Without Breakdown: A Case Study', *The Scientific American*, 75, July, 1952, pp. 31–41; Edward

M. Bruner, 'Urbanization and Ethnic Identity in North Sumatra', *American Anthropologist*, 63, 3, 1961, pp. 508–21; Janet Abu-Lughod, 'Migrant Adjustment to City Life: The Egyptian Case', *American Journal of Sociology*, 67, July, 1961, pp. 22–32, and Philip Mayer, *Townsmen or Tribesmen. Conservatism and the Process of Urbanization*, Capetown, 1962

47. See S. H. Franklin, 'Systems of Production, Systems of Appropriation', *Pacific Viewpoint*, 6, 2, 1965, pp. 145–66

48. Ibid., p. 148

49. Ibid., p. 148

50. Some peasant economies are being penetrated by Socialism (e.g. Poland and China)

51. See Pitirim A. Sorokin, *Social and Cultural Mobility*, Glencoe, Illinois, 1959

52. See Clyde J. Mitchell, 'Theoretical Orientations in African Urban Studies' in M. Banton (ed.), *The Social Anthropology of Complex Societies*, London, 1966, pp. 37–68

53. Ibid., p. 44

54. Ibid., p. 49

55. A. L. Epstein, suggests a modified framework (1) industrial structure (2) civic structure (3) demographic imperative. 'Urbanization and Social Change in Africa', *Current Anthropology*, 8, 4, October, 1967, pp. 275–312

56. See A. Southall, 'Introductory Summary', in A. Southall (ed.), *Social Change in Modern Africa*, London, pp. 1–46. Cited by Mitchell, op. cit., p. 50

57. Mitchell, op. cit., pp. 50–1

58. See William Bascom, 'Urbanism as a Traditional African Pattern', *The Sociological Review*, 7, 1959, pp. 29–43. Cited by Mitchell, op. cit., p. 51

59. A. L. Epstein, *Politics in an Urban African Community*, Manchester, 1958, p. 231

60. Mayer, op. cit., p. 135

The Rural-Urban Continuum Debate:
The Preindustrial City and Rural-Urban
Migration

*Indeed the difficulty of accommodating movement, or process, has
already been noticed as a main limitation of any model that works
solely in terms of situation selection.*[1]

THIS PAPER is an attempt to reformulate the concepts of
the rural–urban continuum and seeks to provide a more adequate conceptual framework for the investigation of rural–
urban migration. There is no attempt to present a report of
work in progress: the paper is purely theoretical. At the same
time, the work which the writer has been carrying out in
recent years investigating rural migrants in one Southeast
Asian city has certainly induced doubts as to the validity of
what has been called '. . . one of the most familiar conceptual
frameworks in sociology'.[2]

The writer is well aware of the fact that in seeking to investigate this question of an adequate definition of rural and urban
society, he is raising a problem which the majority of social
scientists generally feel has been overdiscussed. This attitude
seems to be well summed up by the title of one of the most
influential articles concerning the rural–urban continuum,
'The Rural–Urban Continuum: Real but Relatively Unimportant'.[3] The writer would not dispute the conclusion implicit
in this title that rural–urban differences exist, but he would
question the suggestion that they are of little importance. The
mere fact that the debate over the question of the rural–
urban continuum has produced such a voluminous literature,
as well as the acceptance of the framework as one of the basic

concepts of sociology, and has been included in virtually every sociological textbook, seems to be ample evidence of its importance. This is surely an adequate enough reason to investigate the theoretical foundations of the continuum.

This paper, then, is not concerned with the question of the reality of rural–urban differences, for these are assumed to exist in varying degrees in practically every nation today. What is questioned are the present theoretical models of the rural–urban continuum which are used in the analysis of the real world. Many of the earlier criticisms of the rural–urban continuum are reiterated in this paper, but few of these criticisms have concentrated on the two aspects in which the 'continuum' reveals its greatest weaknesses; its failure to include an adequate classification of urban types, and its complete exclusion of the movement of people from a rural to an urban setting. Thus the three parts of the title neatly tie together the points that are made in this paper: (a) The rural–urban continuum represents the static abstract model used for analysing aspects of the national or world society; (b) the model of the preindustrial city represents the attempt to develop submodels which anticipate development and change and provide historical depth; (c) the acceptance of migration acknowledges the need to build processes into the model of the rural–urban continuum, and points to the limitations of any definition which is solely based on situation. In fact the rural and urban models are simply frameworks within which people can be conceived as moving. People move from the rural to the urban situation and frequently they carry the values and characteristics of the rural situation into the urban situation. Such people can influence, and are also influenced, in an interaction which completely changes the characteristics of the models.

Thus stated, the paper falls into four parts: (i) a description and a discussion of the characteristics of the rural–urban models and the criticisms which have been levelled against them; (ii) the significance of the concept of the pre-industrial city as an attempt to modify one of these models and the importance of recognizing the existence of submodels of urban types; (iii) migration as a mobile factor affecting the validity of these models; (iv) change and mobility will be incorporated into a typology of rural–urban models in an attempt to make them a more valid conceptual framework for formulating and testing hypotheses.

THE RURAL–URBAN CONTINUUM DEBATE[4]

In briefly reviewing the history of the rural–urban continuum, it is unnecessary to trace the history of the literature from its earliest years. This is adequately done in books dealing with the history of urban studies such as those of Sjoberg,[5] Mumford,[6] and in particular Sorokin and Zimmerman's *Principles of Rural–Urban Sociology*.[7] It is sufficient to note that from the earliest times social, political and economic theorists, as well as literary writers, have accepted this distinction between rural and urban. Hesiod's[8] description of early peasant life is as clear in its recognition of the values of rural life as is Plato's[9] praise of the virtues of urban society. The medieval social theorists Ibn Khaldun[10] and Botero[11] stressed these differences between rural and urban society in no less definite a fashion. Shakespeare's drunken rural idiots and his crafty urban rogues were the literary antecedents of the personalities which are said to be found in rural and urban society. It is frequently asserted that rural–urban differences are developing in some kind of unilinear fashion which is leading to a breakdown of rural–urban differences. It may be true that rural–urban differences were less during the earliest periods of the formation of the city, but it seems clear that city and rural life have been remarkably separate since earliest times. The extent of their early relationships still needs much historical research. Even in modern Western society where Sorokin and Zimmerman point out 'there are many reasons to think that the climax of the differentiation between the city and country in the United States and European societies, is already over . . .'[12] there is considerable doubt whether rural–urban differences in habits and attitudes are in fact lessening. Thus Swedner, after an exhaustive study of differences in rural–urban attitudes and habits in south Sweden, reports that such differences still persist. This interpretation of the historical lessening of rural–urban differences such as is shown in Figure 1, should be treated with some scepticism.[13]

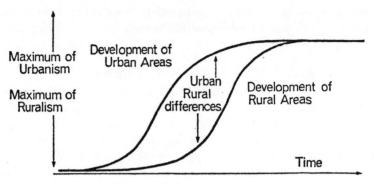

Figure 1. Model of the development of rural and urban areas (after Swedner, 1960)

It is also necessary to avoid the assertion implicit in such a historical process as that described above and accepted by writers such as Beals that 'it is our tentative hypothesis that there is a commonality of process (*by which he refers to urbanization*)* which, if verified by empirical research, will ultimately lead to the development of a common body of concepts and generalizations applicable to an ever-widening body of phenomena'.[14] It seems dangerous to assert that a process will automatically produce a common response whatever the unique cultural or historical elements of society. Although the process of urbanization, i.e. the growth of cities, is a general enough process, a great deal depends on the manner in which a city grows. A city which is growing largely from the in-migration of rural people will have a vastly different character from a city which is growing only from natural increase.

This section of the paper is concerned principally with tracing the history of the distinction between rural and urban societies which has grown up since the industrial revolution, because it is essentially the passing of a moral judgment on the psychological characteristics of city life in the early days of the industrial revolution which has led to the distinction between the psychological characteristics of the rural and urban dwellers which is built into the rural–urban continuum today. Engels' description of psychological characteristics of

* My italics.

the inhabitants of the English industrial towns, 'The dissolution of mankind into monads, of which each one has a separate principle, the world of atoms, is here carried to its utmost extreme',[15] is echoed in Durkheim and in Wirth's classic exposition of the character of the city when he says, 'Wherever large numbers of differently constituted individuals congregate, the process of depersonalisation also enters'.[16] Thus cities become evil things where crime, disorder, personal disorganization are common. It is necessary to dwell at some length on Wirth's definition of the characteristics of the city because portions of it have been accepted as characterizing the model of urban society as opposed to rural society.

Virtually every article on the subject of the rural–urban continuum treats Wirth's article at length. Wirth claimed that

On the basis of the three variables, number, density of settlement, and degree of heterogeneity of the urban population, it appears possible to explain the characteristics of urban life and to account for the differences between cities of various sizes and types.[17]

He then went on to argue that a large number of characteristics of social and political organization were products of these variables. They are responsible for many features of the urban personality which is characterized by reserve, blasé outlook, indifference; sophistication and cosmopolitanism; rationality; relativistic perspectives; tolerant, competitive, self-aggrandizing and exploitative attitudes; feelings of friction, irritation, and nervous tension bred by frustration and other similar characteristics of which the most notable were marked degrees of personal disorganization. In a similar fashion, the social organization of a city was to a large extent conditioned by these three variables: great importance of secondary, rather than primary, contacts; less integrated social organization; pecuniary nexus; greater independence of specialists; less dependence on particular individuals; impersonal, transitory, superficial, segmental and utilitarian social contacts; and exaggerated importance of time.[18]

Wirth's definition of the city has come under criticism from many directions. Many workers in non-Western cities stress the point that a large number of the characteristics of the personality of the urban dweller and his social organization described by Wirth are not found in these cities.[19] This criticism does not, however, invalidate Wirth's model of the Western city at the time he was writing. A more serious argument against the validity of the model is stated by Dewey.[20] He points out that the major criticisms have been with Wirth's choice of independent and dependent variables.

Their looseness has prompted some writers to question the reasonableness of population as the definition's base. Reiss, for one, suggests that, empirically, at least, 'urban' can be independent of size and density. If this is true, then large size and high density of settlement are not always conditions for an urban way of life in any given community.[21]

Similar criticisms have also been directed at the rural pole of the continuum. In discussing the writings on the rural pole of the continuum, it is necessary to distinguish between the American sociologists of the 'twenties and thirties' who were essentially concerned with the rural–urban continuum applied to Western society, and anthropologists such as Redfield who formulated the concept in the context of non-Western society, and coined the term 'a folk-urban continuum'. Sorokin and Zimmerman's[22] clear statements of the rural–urban dichotomy in an exhaustive treatment of the differences between rural and urban societies present virtually every point of distinction between rural and urban societies. It is interesting to note that this work is mentioned but seldom acknowledged by later writers. They also emphasize the need to construct a model type of urban and rural community,[23] drawing the stimulus for the method from Weber. For the ideas on the psychological characteristics of the people of the two models, they draw heavily on the ideas of Simmel, Durkheim and Tonnies.

Redfield, too, drew his ideas from such writers. In a series of field studies in Central America in the 'thirties and forties', he postulated the folk–urban continuum, and admits his indebtedness to these writers who influenced him when he says,

It is not that the few general ideas that occur in these pages are new. The reader of Durkheim will recognize the influence of his contrast between the social segment and the social organ and between the sacred and the profane. There is a strong flavour of Henry Maine about the transition implied in the following pages from the familial society to one emphasizing individual action, and formal political controls. Lewis H. Morgan's opposition of *societas* to *civitas* finds a response in these pages. Tonnies' antithesis between the Gemeinschaft and the Gesellschaft has contributed to the general conceptions which helped formulate the questions asked of the materials in Yucatan.[24]

He then goes on to postulate what he considers the folk–urban continuum, by establishing two types in a similar fashion to Sorokin and Zimmerman.

The characters there asserted to identify the first 'type' (*by which he means folk society*)* are isolation; cultural homogeneity; organization of conventional understandings into a 'single web of interrelated meanings'; adjustment to the local environment; predominant personal character of the relationships; relative importance of familial institutions; relative importance of sacred sanctions as compared with secular; development of ritual expression of belief and attitude; tendency for much of the behaviour of the individual to involve his familial or local group. . . . The line of thought suggested by the discovery or creation of these 'types' leads to some hypotheses: (1) the primitive and peasant societies (which will be found to be, as compared with other societies, isolated and homogeneous local communities) have in general characters of the first type. (2) When such societies undergo contact and communication with urbanized society (or at least with modern Western urbanized society), they tend to change in the direction of the opposite of these characters.[25]

Redfield continued his concern with the folk pole of the continuum and did not define the urban model to such an extent. In fact, the urban model was assumed to be the opposite to the folk model. Despite considerable criticism Redfield continued to emphasize this model of the folk–urban continuum in his remaining field studies, and in a series of theoretical works culminating in *Peasant Society and Culture*.[26] It is true that he did respond to some of this criticism by modifying his models of

* My italics.

folk society in two ways. First, he broke down his model of folk society so that he distinguished between precivilized and civilized communities.[27] He also distinguished between folk societies and peasant societies: 'The folk society may be conceived as that imagined combination of societal elements which would characterize a long-established, isolated and non-literate integral self-contained community; the folk society is that society seen as a system of common understandings.'[28] Peasant societies, on the other hand, were those societies where 'Agriculture is a livelihood and a way of life, not a business for profit.'[29] There were 'part-societies' which existed in relationship to market centres and towns. Secondly, he did attempt to investigate the relationship of folk society and the city more closely in his studies of the relationship of the Great and Little Tradition.

But the key to Redfield's distinction between the city and the folk society and the point on which he never recanted is the moral nature of the two societies. He says: 'It may be repeated that the folk society is that society in which the technical order is subordinated within the moral order. The moral order is there, self-consistent and strong.'[30] In the city '. . . prevailing common understandings have to do with the technical not the moral order. . .'.[31] Thus Redfield's definition tied him to the tradition of the early Western sociologists and the Wirth-type definition of the Western city, even though he was concerned with formulating the definition of the folk-urban continuum in a non-Western context.[32]

This hasty sketch of the main hypotheses of the rural–urban continuum has dwelt at some length on what is regarded as the key to the distinction between rural and urban society by these writers—the opposed moral nature of these two societies—because this definition has been accepted almost universally by later writers. Towns are thus thought to be crucibles of cultural and social change. Not only does change occur in the cities, but it flows outward from them, bringing about change in the countryside. The towns are '. . . solvents, weakening traditional social ties and loosening the hold of traditional beliefs and values'.[33] Such conceptual frameworks, which stem directly from the models of rural and urban society created by Wirth and Redfield, dominate practically all research into rural–urban differences.

But these models have by no means been uniformly accepted. A review of the criticisms is best accomplished within the framework of the critique presented by Redfield's chief critic, Oscar Lewis.[34] Lewis's first criticism is that 'The folk–urban conceptualization of social change focuses attention primarily on the city as the source of change, to the exclusion or neglect of other factors of an internal or external nature',[35] and he points to the incorporation of Spanish rural elements, such as the plough, as increasing the heterogeneity of rural culture. Steward is also critical of Redfield's theories:

> Redfield did not attempt to conceptualize suprafolk levels of socio-cultural integration, but in his studies of Yucatan he uses the urban society as a contrasting type. Subjected to urbanization, the folk society is secularized, individualized, and disorganized. Urbanization, however, is but one of the processes through which a folk society may be integrated into a larger socio-cultural system; for cities are but specialized parts of such systems. Some folk societies are incorporated into states and nations as regionally specialized sub-cultures which do not undergo urbanization at all and which are readapted rather than transformed.[36]

The defence of Redfield has been largely taken up by Miner who suggests that although Redfield 'does neglect other sources of change than urban contact, we cannot agree that the folk–urban continuum excludes other conceptualization'.[37] Beals also points to the fact that the express aim of Redfield's work was the concern 'with the way in which the influence of urbanism is extended into the urban hinterland and particularly into the folk cultures'.[38] Thus stated, Redfield does not stand condemned for not carrying out the professed aims of his research. He can, however, be criticized for inadequate field-work in not viewing the process of rural and urban contact as a two-way process in which both societies can influence the other. The main problem is that once the model of the rural–urban continuum, with its fallacious assumptions of the nature of rural and urban society, is created, it becomes rather like an institution—self-perpetuating and not to be criticized.

43

Lewis's second major criticism of Redfield concerns the moral order he attributes to folk societies. He says:

> Underlying the folk–urban dichotomy as used by Redfield, is a system of value judgments which contains the old Rousseauan notion of primitive people as noble savages, and the corollary that with civilization has come the fall of man. . . . It is assumed that all folk societies are integrated while urban societies are the great disorganizing force.[39]

This criticism then accuses Redfield of using false value judgments in his field-work, which have led him to view the moral nature of peasant society in a completely false light. It is significant that this is the only one of Lewis's criticisms that Redfield replied to at any length. It is indicative, perhaps, of the emphasis he placed on the moral nature of peasant society. His reply is a skilful evasion rather than a carefully argued response. He does not deny that Lewis had 'established the objective truth of certain of the unpleasant features of Tepoztecan (Tepoztlan) life',[40] but in reply claims that his book was not an attempt at a rounded study. 'Indeed, I expressly disclaimed that it was; I thought of it as a statement of one phase of a complex truth.'[41] He argues that the personal approach of the field-worker must be taken into account: 'There are hidden questions behind the two books that have been written about Tepoztlan. The hidden question behind my book is "What do these people enjoy?" The hidden question behind Dr. Lewis' book is, "What do these people suffer from?"'[42] Finally in another text Redfield reiterates a point that he made earlier; the right of the fieldworker to make value judgments about the society in which he works.

> Perhaps we should ask the field ethnologist not that he divest himself of values, for that is impossible, nor that he emphasize in every case values predominating in his own times with regard to applied science, increased production and adjusted personalities, but that he make plain what he does find good or bad about the people he reports.[43]

Thus, Redfield's reply is no real answer to Lewis' criticisms. He admits that Lewis has established that his picture of Tepoztlan life was incomplete, arguing that he was not attempting to produce anything more than a 'statement of one phase of a complex truth'. But, on the other hand, he made no attempt to reformulate his model of folk society. Thus the folk–urban continuum has been perpetuated in this false fashion.

The other criticisms which Lewis makes are primarily concerned with the validity of the model of the folk–urban continuum which Miner has described as concerning 'The Problem of Fit'.[44] It is here, too, that the majority of other writers have criticized the continuum. The problem concerns how useful the theoretical model of the continuum is in the analysis of the real world. The criticism of the model from this point of view can be divided into three broad groups: (i) criticism of the duality of the model; that is the assumption that the characteristics of one of the poles is the reverse of the other pole, as for example in the organization–disorganization paired variable; (ii) criticism of the model because of its failure to approximate reality; (iii) criticisms of either end of the continuum—the rural or the urban poles.

(i) *Criticism of the duality of the model.* The criticisms of the use of paired hypotheses in the model are numerous. A major point of issue is that the paired hypotheses such as rural and urban or organization and disorganization rarely vary together. Thus, for instance, rural elements are often found in an urban setting. Lewis found that the organization–disorganization hypothesis was not true in his study of migrants in Mexico City,[45] and many other criticisms have been levelled at this aspect of the continuum. A second criticism is that the introduction of polar concepts does not allow for any type of scale between the two poles. Thus the social structure of people in a city is always disorganized while that of people in the rural areas is always organized. There is never a case of people who are partly disorganized or partly organized. As Janet Abu-Lughod says: 'In short, according to the rural–urban dichotomy, a hypothetical villager is to be dropped, unarmed, into the heart of urban Cairo to assimilate or perish. He is to be granted no cushions to soften his fall.'[46] Such a situation is patently false in the majority of Asian, African and South American cities today. The most serious theoretical attempt to justify the use of paired concepts such as the rural–urban

45

continuum has come from Bendix and Berger who suggest that 'paired concepts are attempts to conceptualize what we know about the range of variability of social phenomena so that we are enabled to deal abstractly with their known extremes, regardless of whether we focus on the levels of interactions, of institutions, or of societies as wholes'.[47] The justification of paired concepts is that they are a methodological formulation of 'the fact that concrete human relationships are ambiguous'.[48] There is a necessity to keep these concepts because they prevent undue bias creeping into both concept formulation and testing. Despite Bendix and Berger's defence, it seems obvious that the weakness of the use of paired hypotheses in the model of rural and urban society is that they lead to situations where everything is black or white, rural or urban, and thus introduce faulty thinking into the investigation of rural–urban differences.

(ii) *Criticism of the model because of its failure to approximate reality.* Much of this criticism overlaps to some extent with the other categories of criticism. Its distinctiveness is largely due to the fact that it has come from fieldworkers who have been investigating rural–urban differences in non-Western environments. Thus Edward Bruner's work amongst the Toba Batak in Medan, Sumatra, leads him to state: 'It is clear that the social concomitants of the transition from rural to urban life are not the same in South-East Asia as in Western society.'[49] Janet Abu-Lughod remarks even more dogmatically, on the basis of her field-work amongst rural migrants in Cairo City, that 'It is our contention here that the dichotomy is as invalid in Egypt and in many other newly awakening nations as it is in the Western nations. . .'.[50] My own conclusions on migrants in Kuala Lumpur City would support such conclusions. The point here is that the model of rural–urban differences does not seem to stand up to cross-cultural comparisons. As Sjoberg has said, 'With respect to rural–urban differences, many of the generalizations resulting from the early influences of Wirth and Redfield, among others, reflected in today's sociology textbooks, require a thorough overhauling. Numerous patterns on the American scene are erroneously thought to hold for other societies as well. . . .'[51]

Redfield defends himself well on this count. He argues that as such models are simply mental constructs, they cannot be attacked from the point of view of their failure to approximate reality. He says,

> In various publications I have attempted to describe the model of the primitive small society for which Margaret Mead finds use even in the study of something that is very different from it: the group characters of modern national states. I tried to make explicit the abstract and general qualities of that society and culture that can be imagined to be more isolated, more self-contained, than is even the Andamanese band. Once this description was on paper, other students of particular real societies forming part of civilizations and national states made the indicated comparisons between this model and the peasant communities in which they worked. What they noticed was, of course, the differences. The Mexican or Brazilian village was not, in many ways, like the abstract model. In not a few cases the students drew the conclusion that the model was wrong. I would rather say that the abstraction, being, as Mead says, a 'conceptual model', cannot be wrong. It does not describe any particular real society. It is there to point the way to the study of that which its use brings to notice.[52]

The question which arises is, however, how often a model can be modified from studies of reality before it loses its validity as a research tool. Bendix and Berger argue that writers of the critiques are as much to blame as the makers of the models, because they have not distinguished 'between concept formation and the formulation and testing of hypotheses. In cases where such critiques are justified, it would be necessary to replace the discarded with a new concept, which is more serviceable.'[53] In the conclusion to this paper such a set of new concepts is put forward in the hope that they will prove to be a more adequate model of rural and urban societies.

(iii) *Criticisms of either end of the continuum; the rural or the urban poles.* The discussion earlier in the paper has to some extent dealt with the criticisms which have been made of the rural pole of the continuum and, therefore, it is intended to concentrate on the criticisms of the urban pole of the model. It must be noted that, although Redfield responded to the criticism of his model of folk society by introducing submodels of rural society, there was no corresponding attempt to modify the urban model. This is rather surprising, for one of Lewis' most trenchant criticisms was that the urban pole was 'too much of a "catch-all" to be useful for cultural analysis. . . . What we need to know is what kind of urban society, under what conditions of contact, and a host of other specific historical data.'[54] Hoselitz has also criticized this aspect of the continuum, commenting that Redfield's schema does not penetrate the differences between urban centres.[55] It seems necessary, therefore, to create submodels of the urban pole if any adequate conceptual framework can be constructed to encompass rural–urban differences.

THE PREINDUSTRIAL CITY

This creates the problem of constructing some adequate and meaningful set of models of urban society. Hoselitz is pessimistic of the possibilities of constructing ideal models of urban society. 'The difficulty in constructing even an ideal-type model of urban culture is due to that fact that its outstanding characteristic is its heterogeneity and that, therefore, sets of culture traits found in the urban centres of one country need not be repeated in those of another country.'[56] Despite this difficulty many attempts have been made to arrive at a classification of cities, particularly by geographers.[57] In general, however, their efforts have been largely concentrated on attempting to classify cities on the basis of criteria such as size and economic function, and they have not been concerned with attempting to build up a total model of the various types of cities. A recent publication of Gideon Sjoberg[58] has classified cities on the basis of their economic, social, ecological and political characteristics in a much more comprehensive fashion. While this book has been heavily criticized because of the inaccuracy of historical data,[59] the division which the writer makes between preindustrial cities and industrial cities has not received as much criticism. Sjoberg argues that, 'Our principal hypothesis is that in their structure, or form, preindustrial cities—whether in medieval Europe, traditional China, India, or elsewhere—resemble one another closely and in turn differ markedly from modern industrial–urban centres.'[60] The preindustrial city which Sjoberg describes is a constructed type, and its characteristics are strikingly different from the modern industrial–urban city. Cities of this type have existed from probably 4000 B.C., and they still continue today in the form of a city such as Mecca. The population of these cities is small, seldom 'ranging over 100,000'; the spatial arrangement of the city is dominated by the significance of the city's centre as 'the hub of governmental and religious activity more than of commercial ventures'. Around this centre the elite groups' residences are concentrated and the lower class and outcaste groups are relegated to the cities' periphery; ethnic separation was at a maximum; multiple functions are characteristic of site utilization; the class structure was marked and there is little opportunity for social mobility; the large extended family with numerous relatives residing in one household is the key socialization agency in the community; there is a sharp differentiation between the sexes, the men lording it over the women; economic activity is poorly developed and the most common form of economic organization is the guild, typically community-bound; little standardization is found in prices or currency and the marketing procedure is consequently fluid; the political structure is dominated by the upper-class, who hold all the key governmental posts; the sovereign leaders base their authority upon appeals to tradition and to absolutes; similar rigid hierarchical patterns are found in religion and education; religion is highly important and the day-by-day behaviour of the people is largely governed by religious injunctions.[61] These, then, are some of the patterns which characterize the model of the preindustrial city and which provide a striking contrast to the features of the industrial city as outlined by Wirth. It is obvious that this type of city exerted a very different type of attraction to the industrial city in terms of rural–urban migration. Because the cities were often 'orthogenetic' cities, people from the countryside would often flood into the cities at times of religious or political ceremonies and festivals. During periods of political strife rural people would also move to cities for protection, but this was generally only a temporary migration from which people would return to rural areas. Rural people seldom moved to such cities because of the economic attraction of jobs and thus such cities grew generally from natural increase.[62]

Perhaps the greatest fault of Sjoberg's twofold division of cities is that he has failed to take account of cities that have grown as links in the interaction of two civilizations. Such towns were flourishing even in the preindustrial society; for example, as a result of the contact of the Roman Empire and the North African cultures. Such cities are probably distinct enough to deserve a category of their own. They might be aptly titled 'colonial cities'.

In attempting to construct a model of the 'colonial city' there are considerable difficulties. Colonial towns showed many variations in structure or form depending upon the form of colonial impact. For instance, in areas, such as Australia or North America, where there was no history of indigenous urban settlement and permanent settler populations of colonists were established, the colonial towns can be labelled 'replica towns', in that the colonists attempted to establish urban settlements which were replicas of their homeland. While this type is of considerable importance, it is the towns which grew up in the period since 1800 in the tropical areas of Africa and Asia which are perhaps the best example of the 'colonial city'. These towns were broadly of three types: (i) Those towns which represent a mixture of the industrial city and the pre-industrial city. Frequently, as in Kano, they were administrative centres of the indigenous societies and a colonial administrative structure was grafted on to the already existing preindustrial city. (ii) The towns which were connected with the exploitation of minerals, such as Luanshya in Central Africa, which were wholly industrial in nature. (iii) The large port towns which acted as the receiving and exporting centres for the colonial empires.

The latter were perhaps the most ubiquitous. Such cities often possessed a considerable proportion of the urban population of the colony, and there was no graded hierarchy of cities from large to small as in Western countries. Hauser has described this characteristic in Southeast Asia: '. . . as a result of the colonial heritage, many of the countries of Asia, and especially Southeast Asia . . . are characterized by one great metropolis, "the primate city", a great city which dominates the urban situation.'[63] Such cities were brought into existence to satisfy the needs of commerce[64] and are represented by the great, sprawling 'agglomérations urbaines'[65] which grew up as the great exporting and importing centres of the colonial empires. In such towns the long, ugly tin warehouses replaced the industrial smokestacks of the industrial towns of Europe. Yet such cities were characterized by a political and social structure which was no less hierarchical than the preindustrial city. The colonial administrator and businessman was alien from those he administered, and there was virtually no entry from the indigenous groups into the ranks of the administrators. This, then, was a stratified society similar in pattern to that of the preindustrial city. 'The city was a grouping of communities, each of which carried on its pattern of life in a different way. Thus the old patterns of economic organization in the form of guilds persisted side by side with the "rational" organization of production of goods, with expediential relations between buyer and seller. . . .'[66] The elite group residences tended to concentrate around the hub of governmental and religious activity, but each community concentrated around the centre of its activities. Economically the cities, because they largely concentrated on commerce, had an occupational structure which was characterized by a marked development of the tertiary sector; and the cities, although they became important educational, commercial and political centres, seldom attracted rural migrants to the extent of the industrial cities of nineteenth-century Europe. These tentative characteristics of the colonial city are enough to justify its creation as a distinct model. Thus three models of urban society—the preindustrial city, the colonial city, and the industrial city—can be put forward and when linked with a threefold grouping of rural society; namely, 'folk', 'peasant', and 'farmer' societies,[67] a much more plausible model of rural–urban differences can be constructed. The knowledge of each of these models' particular characteristics, if established carefully, could greatly aid the more accurate investigation of the rural–urban differences, the process of rural–urban migration, or the extension of urban influences into rural areas.

MIGRATION

One of the last remaining criticisms of the rural–urban continuum, to reiterate the point made at the beginning of this paper, is the fact that the model does not take into account the movement of people from the rural pole to the urban pole. Such movements bring people whose values, habits and attitudes and whose political, economic and social organization are those of the rural areas into urban areas where they contrast sharply with the urban society. For instance, the majority of Malays in Kuala Lumpur City are politically organized within a framework which is identical with that of rural areas.[68] Such aspects of rural society do not necessarily disappear in the urban environment, especially when the number of rural migrants is large, and in many of the cities of the world today the number of rural migrants is strikingly large. This is hardly surprising because the majority of the countries of the world are characterized by rapid urbanization. In particular this is true of the predominantly agricultural countries, where, although the percentage of people living in urban centres is still small, extremely rapid urbanization is occurring.[69] Although these cities are growing to some extent from natural increase, the striking fact from the point of view of this paper is that much of this growth is greatly aided by migration from rural areas. Janet Abu-Lughod reports that in Cairo in 1950: 'More than one-third of the permanent residents of Cairo have been born outside the city.'[70] A survey carried out in Baghdad during 1956–7 found that 57 per cent of the respondents had been born outside the city.[71] In Asia similar patterns also occur. In a survey conducted in Djakarta in 1954, over 75 per cent of the household heads were born outside the city. This figure is unduly high and possibly reflects two sources of error. First, the fact that it is customary for women living in the city to return to their home village to give birth to their children. Secondly, that the survey concentrated unduly in areas in which the migrants lived.[72] In India where 'it has been widely accepted that the rural population . . . is comparatively non-migratory, because it is too strongly tied to its village origins by bonds of kinship, marriage customs, language, and centuries of ingroup living to be easily diverted to the comparative insecurity and strangeness of the city',[73] the rate of net in-migration into the cities between 1941 and 1951 was equivalent to 20 per cent of the 1941 urban population.[74] In some of the larger cities the proportion of rural migrants in the city was much larger and Bogue reports that rural–urban migration 'has now progressed to a point where the residents of almost every village have relatives or fellow villagers living in at least one (and possibly several) of the major cities'.[75]

In Latin America rural–urban migration contributes a much greater component of the population increase of the cities. The Population Branch of the Bureau of Social Affairs, United Nations, reports that 'in most of the countries under considera-tion . . . in the last interval between censuses internal migration contributed half and in some instances even as much as two-thirds of the increase of the urban population'.[76] During the last intercensual period the range varied from as much as 71 per cent of the urban growth in Venezuela to 26 per cent in Cuba. Similar patterns have also been reported in Africa, where the number of rural in-migrants in towns is very high, especially in the industrial centres of the Central and Southern Africa.[77]

The implications of this flood of rural migrants to the town to any model of the rural–urban continuum are obvious. The majority of the world's cities are going through a period of 'ruralization' which is blunting rather than sharpening the distinction between rural and urban. What is more, it seems unlikely that these differences will ever sharpen as greatly as they did in the West, because the improvements in technology and communications (extensions of roads, education, radio, and films) means that aspects of the urban society can be extended into rural areas. This process has been vividly portrayed in Lerner's description of the changes which occurred in the small Turkish village of Balgat,[78] and in many other studies. Thus the picture which Davis paints of the flow of migrants from country-side to city in Africa, as corresponding to 'a rapid transition telescoping several millennia into a short span',[79] though probably truer of Africa than elsewhere, is everywhere breaking down. 'Peasants now want to be something other than peasants.'[80] The extension of education into rural areas is creating a peasant who is more willing to migrate. Bogue, after considerable research in India, says that 'the propensity to migrate to urban areas is much higher among literate and educated people than among the illiterate, and that as the level of education rises the tendency to travel greater distances to seek employment increases'.[81] Radio, films, and faster transport are producing a peasant who is more knowledgeable about the urban environment. The frequently attributed causes of rural out-migration, such as population pressure, lack of land and underemployment still exist, but the pull factors are increasingly becoming important. The city, even though it does not always offer improved economic status, seems to exert some magical pull on the rural migrant. Factors of a more personal kind than mere economic motivation are in operation. The migrant frequently leaves his home because he is dissatisfied with the traditional environment; for some, the trip to the city is a 'modern form of initiation rite; a youth cannot expect to win a girl's favours unless he can show the brand of town upon him'.[82] Others are summoned to the city by relatives who are already there and promise education and jobs, and others leave because the traditional environment does not give the young and aspiring man the opportunity to succeed in obtaining authority. These migrants are 'innovating' migrants,[83] who are moving to the city as much for the new opportunities it offers as to escape from the limitations of their traditional environment.[84]

The motivations forcing the rural migrant to the city are many and influence him greatly in his reaction to the city, but in addition, the values and culture of the migrant are of no less importance. Thus, the manner in which the rural migrant adjusts to the city depends on the migrant, his motivations, his dreams, and his culture.[85] It also depends on the type of rural society from which the migrant comes, and the type of city to which he moves. Thus the African tribesman who moves from a tribal society to an industrial city will in all probability find it harder to adjust to the urban environment than would a peasant moving to a similar industrial city. The one important factor that may help the rural migrant in making a better adjustment to the urban environment is the number of his fellow rural migrants who are in the city, for he can be helped in the process of adjusting to the city by associating with his fellow rural migrants. Frequently rural patterns and institutions persist as the rural migrant finds it easier to 'accommodate'[86] than assimilate to the urban way of life. Philip Mayer would carry this argument even further, claiming that the results of his research amongst Bantu migrants in East London indicates that some migrants never become completely urban no matter how long they live in the town.[87] The researcher into rural–urban differences in the non-Western countries too often fails to see that the elements he finds in the city, such as high-fertility, and the persistence of the extended family which he associates with the rural environment, are simply aspects of the 'ruralness' of cities. Whether, with the passing of time and the tendencies of cities to grow more from natural increase, they will disappear and be replaced by social and personality patterns which are more characteristic of the Western city, is a question which cannot as yet be answered.

How then can this factor of 'ruralization' of the cities be incorporated into the typology of urban models so that they will be a more accurate group of models with which to investigate reality?[88] Of course, it may be argued that 'ruralization' is simply a sub-part of the process of 'urbanization'. If the purely physical definition of urbanization as the process of the physical growth of cities is accepted, then ruralization is part of urbanization because it does involve the movement of people from rural to urban areas. If, however, the wider definition of urbanization as a process which sees the urban area as providing an environment in which social, economic and psychological changes inevitably occur is accepted, it may be then argued that the swamping of cities by large numbers of rural migrants produces a situation in which they are too numerous for the supposedly deterministic qualities of the urban area to operate. The danger is, of course, that 'ruralization' will acquire the same deterministic qualities as 'urbanization'. This, however, is not meant. It is simply claimed that when a city has a high number of rural migrants, it has a high number of features which are characteristically rural. This does not mean that the features of an urban style of life are affected, but it does mean that any static model of urbanism must be changed.

Taeuber has provided a useful definition of cities which would encompass the problem of rural migrants forming a sizeable percentage of the city's population when she defined Japanese cities as either 'stable' or 'migrant' cities.[89] Migrant cities are those cities growing substantially from the in-migration of rural migrants, stable cities those cities which are either declining, stable, or growing from natural increase. This group would also include cities which are growing from the movement of people from smaller urban areas. Thus, for instance, in the United States the largest urban areas are growing from both natural increase and movement from other urban areas. Rural migration is contributing less and less to urban growth.[90] The question is where to make the cutoff point in the percentage of migrants born in rural areas in order to define a migrant city. One of the features of migration to towns appears to be 'step-migration', a pattern in which migrants move from a rural area to a smaller town and then finally to a larger town. Evidence is presented for this type of migration in India by Hoselitz.[91] Thus, smaller and more provincial towns are more likely to be classified as migrant towns. It is tentatively suggested that if 40 per cent of the population over 10 years of age is born in rural areas, it should be defined as a migrant city.[92] Yet another addition to this classification could be some attempt to incorporate various types of migrants. Taeuber's distinction between stable and migrant cities based on place of birth alone is a crude one. A useful refinement could be achieved by classifying migrants according to whether or not they have characteristics typical of urban-born persons such as a high literacy rate and a low fertility rate. This modification would rest upon detailed information pertaining to the characteristics of migrants which is noticeably sparse. Most cities will, of course, be migrant cities for only short periods of their growth, but this does not lessen the need to recognize this characteristic in any set of models of rural and urban society.

CONCLUSION

This dual classification of cities can then be added to the

set of models of rural and urban society already suggested and grouped in a typology as illustrated in Figure 2.

This grouping of models is, of course, only tentative and will need a much more careful enumeration of their distinguishing characteristics before it can be used as an aid to the formulation

		URBAN MODELS		
		Preindustrial	Colonial	Industrial
		(These three models of urban society can be either "stable" or "migrant" cities)		
RURAL MODELS	Folk			
	Peasant			
	Farmer			

Figure 2. A typology of rural and urban societies

of detailed hypotheses. But even in this rather simple form the typology of rural and urban models presents a far more realistic theoretical framework to aid in the investigation of both rural and urban differences and rural–urban migration.

Its advantages over the more simple rural–urban continuum are numerous. For instance, the typology of models has no unilinear pattern of historical evolution built into its framework. Thus preindustrial cities, industrial cities, folk and farmer societies can exist within the same nation, and the acceptance of their coexistence makes the explanation of rural–urban differences far more logical. Such a set of models, also, does not necessarily assume a historical lessening of rural–urban differences. The fact that a people in a farmer society and an industrial city have access to very much the same form of education and radio communication does not automatically mean that this will lead to any lessening of the differences in rural–urban attitudes. It is perhaps logical to assume that the psychological differences between the majority of inhabitants

57

of the industrial city and a folk society are greater than those between the inhabitants of the industrial cities and the farmer rural society, but the differences of the former are certainly no greater than between the peasantry and the elite group of the preindustrial city. This set of models also avoids placing undue emphasis on one model as the source of change which could be generated as the result of one rural model to another. A rural society can very clearly change the character of the city as it clearly is doing during the present phase of the 'ruralization' of many of the world's cities. The city, then, is not the sole source of change; simply one element in change.

Duality and paired hypotheses find no place in this grouping of models. The elements of the preindustrial city's distinctiveness are not inevitably linked with the 'folk' society. The two models do frequently coexist, but there is no emphasis on the opposition of their characteristics. Thus the 'migrant' industrial city logically has many characteristics of the peasant society because so many of its inhabitants are from rural areas. The set of models in addition provides a much more adequate framework for cross-cultural analysis. Thus the problems of adjustment to the urban environment which face many rural migrants to the city will be probably greater for folk migrants in the industrial city than for farmer migrants in industrial cities. It is true, of course, that cultural distinctiveness of the cities to which they are migrating may affect the validity of these hypotheses, but no doubt adequate typologies could be developed which could take into account the differences in cross-nation migration, as well as internal migration.

This paper then has attempted to follow the advice of Bendix and Berger by replacing the old conceptual framework of the rural–urban continuum with one that is more serviceable. In a period when anthropological, sociological and geographical research is increasingly focusing upon the phenomena of urbanization in non-Western countries, it is surely important that new conceptual models from which hypotheses are drawn to be tested in the field should be developed to cope with this new orientation of research. It is surprising that it has taken so long for such a new conceptual framework to be suggested.

NOTES

1. Philip Mayer, 'Migrancy and the Study of Africans in Towns', *American Anthropologist*, Vol. 64, January, 1962, p. 589

2. William Petersen, *Population*, 1961, p. 181

3. See Richard Dewey, 'The Rural–Urban Continuum: Real but Relatively Unimportant', *The American Journal of Sociology*, Vol. LXVI, No. 1, July, 1960, pp. 60–6

4. Many of these criticisms of the rural–urban continuum run parallel to those presented by Francisco Benet. However, it is still felt that the criticisms presented in this paper should be aired because of their relevance to the latter part of the paper where a new set of models for rural and urban phenomenon is suggested. See Francisco Benet, 'Sociology Uncertain: The Ideology of the Rural–Urban Continuum', *Comparative Studies in Society and History*, Vol. VI, 1963, October, pp. 1–23. For a recent clash over the validity of the rural–urban continuum see R. E. Paul, 'The Rural–Urban Continuum', *Sociologica Ruralis*, Vol. VI, Nos. 3–4, 1966, pp. 299–327 and by the same author 'The Rural–Urban Continuum. A Reply to Eugeun Lupri', *Sociologica Ruralis*, Vol. VII, No. 1, 1967, pp. 20–8. Eugeun Lupri, 'The Rural–Urban Variable Reconsidered: The Cross-Cultural Perspective', *Sociologica Ruralis*, Vol. VII, No. 1, 1967, pp. 1–20. See also W. D. McTaggart, 'The Reality of Urbanism', *Pacific Viewpoint*, Vol. 6, No. 2, September, 1965, pp. 220–4 for a critique of my paper.

5. See Gideon Sjoberg, *The Preindustrial City: Past and Present*, 1960

6. See Lewis Mumford, *The City in History: Its origins, its transformations, and its prospects*, 1961

7. Pitirim Sorokin and Carle C. Zimmerman, *Principles of Rural–Urban Sociology*, 1929

8. Cited in Robert Redfield, *Peasant Society and Culture*, 1961, pp. 60–79

9. See Plato (trs. Benjamin Jowett.), *The Republic*, 1946

10. Ibn Khaldun (trs. C. Issawi), 'Prologomena' in *An Arab Philosophy of History*, 1960

11. Giovanni Botero (trs. Robert Peterson), 'The Greatness of Cities' in *The Reason of the State and the Greatness of Cities*, 1956

12. Pitirim Sorokin and Carle C. Zimmerman, op. cit., p. 611

13. See Harold Swedner, 'Ecological Differentiation of Habits and Attitudes', *Lund Studies in Sociology*, 1960, p. 3

14. Ralph L. Beals, 'Urbanism, Urbanization and Acculturation' in Olen E. Leonard and Charles P. Loomis (eds.), *Readings in Latin American Social Organization and Institutions*, 1953, p. 170

15. F. Engels (trs. F. K. Wischnewetzky), *Conditions of the Working-Class in England in 1844*, 1952, p. 24

16. Louis Wirth, 'Urbanism as a Way of Life' in Paul K. Hatt and Albert J. Reiss Jr. (eds.), *Cities and Society*, 1959, p. 57

17. Ibid., p. 58

18. Ibid., pp. 60–2
19. See, for instance, Philip M. Hauser's comments in *Urbanization in Asia and the Far East*, 1957
20. See Dewey, op. cit., p. 62
21. Albert J. Reiss, quoted by Dewey, ibid., p. 62
22. See Sorokin and Zimmerman, op. cit.
23. Ibid., p. 15
24. Robert Redfield, *The Folk Culture of Yucatan*, 1941, p. x
25. Ibid., p. 343
26. See Robert Redfield, *Peasant Society and Culture*, 1961
27. See Robert Redfield, *The Primitive World and its Transformations*, 1953
28. Robert Redfield and Milton B. Singer, 'The Cultural Role of Cities', *Economic Development and Cultural Change*, Vol. III, No. I, 1954, pp. 53–73
29. Robert Redfield, op. cit., 1961, p. 18
30. Robert Redfield, op. cit., 1953, p. 48
31. Robert Redfield and Milton B. Singer, op. cit., 1954, p. 57
32. At a later stage, Redfield, did make a dual definition of the city, distinguishing between orthogenetic cities and heterogenetic cities. However, no attempt was made to build this into the 'folk–urban' continuum.
33. Thomas Hodgkin, *Nationalism in Colonial Africa*, 1947, p. 63
34. See Oscar Lewis, *Life in a Mexican Village: Tepoztlan Restudied*, 1951
35. Ibid., p. 432
36. Julian H. Steward, *The Theory of Culture Change—The Methodology of Multilinear Evolution*, 1955, p. 53
37. Horace Miner, 'The Folk–Urban Continuum', in Paul K. Hatt and Albert J. Reiss Jr. (eds.), *Cities and Society 1959*, pp. 22–34
38. Ralph L. Beals, 'Urbanism, Urbanization and Acculturation' in Olen E. Leonard and Charles P. Loomis (eds.), *Readings in Latin American Social Organization and Institutions*, 1953, pp. 167–72
39. Oscar Lewis, op. cit., 1951, p. 435
40. Robert Redfield, *The Little Community*, 1961, p. 134
41. Ibid., p. 135
42. Ibid., p. 136
43. Robert Redfield, op. cit., 1953, p. 156
44. Horace Miner, op. cit., 1959, p. 30
45. Oscar Lewis, 'Urbanization Without Breakdown: A Case Study', *The Scientific American*, No. 75, July, 1952, pp. 31–41
46. Janet Abu-Lughod, 'Migrant Adjustment to City Life: The Egyptian Case', *American Journal of Sociology*, Vol. LXVII, 1961, p. 23
47. Reinhard Bendix and Bennett Berger, 'Images of Society and Problems

of Concept Formation in Sociology' in Llewellyn Gross (ed.), *Symposium on Sociological Theory*, 1959, p. 98

48. Ibid., p. 99

49. Edward M. Bruner, 'Urbanization and Ethnic Identity in North Sumatra', *American Anthropologist*, Vol. 63, No. 1, 1961, p. 508

50. Janet Abu-Lughod, op. cit., 1961, p. 23

51. Gideon Sjoberg, *The Preindustrial City Past and Present*, Glencoe, Illinois, 1960, p. 14–15

52. Robert Redfield, *Peasant Society and Culture*, Chicago, 1961, p. 11

53. Reinhard Bendix and Bennett Berger, 1969, op. cit., p. 114

54. Oscar Lewis, 1951, op. cit., p. 434

55. See Bert F. Hoselitz, *Sociological Aspects of Economic Growth*, Glencoe, Illinois, p. 177

56. Ibid., p. 177

57. See, for instance, Chauncy Harris, 'A Functional Classification of Cities in the United States', *Geographical Review*, 33, January, 1943, pp. 86–99. Sjoberg, 1960, op. cit., p. 10, notes that Marxist writers divide cities into four types 'as a special stage in an inevitable evolutionary process that all societies undergo. For them, the four stages of urban development are the slave-owning city, the feudal city, the capitalist city, and the socialist city.' Redfield and Singer, 1954, op. cit., pp. 53–77, have attempted to divide cities on the basis of their cultural role. Thus they have divided cities into those of orthogenetic nature which were primarily political, religious and administrative centres concerned with carrying the culture of a country forward, and those cities of heterogenetic nature which were largely devoted to trade.
    In this paper the models of rural and urban society which are presented might legitimately have included a fourth type of rural and urban society, i.e. the socialized peasant society, and the socialist city, but they have not been incorporated.

58. Gideon Sjoberg, 1960, op. cit.

59. See for instance, Sylvia L. Thrupp, 'The Creativity of Cities', *Comparative Studies in Society and History*, IV, 1, November, 1961, pp. 60–3 and Paul Wheatley, 'What the Greatness of the City was Said to be', *Pacific Viewpoint*, 4, 2, September, 1963, pp. 163–88 for two exceptionally critical reviews.

60. Gideon Sjoberg, 1960, op. cit., pp. 4–5

61. Summarized from Sjoberg, 1960, pp. 321–8

62. There is much need for research into this pattern of rural–urban relations during the preindustrial period. Hsia-Tung Fei, *China's Gentry: Essays in Rural–Urban Relations*, Chicago, 1953, is an important pioneer study.

63. Philip M. Hauser, 1957, op. cit., pp. 86–7

64. This does not, of course, make such cities distinct. Many of the preindustrial cities were commercial cities, e.g. Bruges, Lübeck or early Canton, as are many industrial cities today.

65. Thomas Hodgkin, 1957, op. cit., p. 64

66. Robert Redfield and Milton B. Singer, 1954, op. cit., 59

67. The characteristics of these models of rural societies are not described in detail in this paper. The earlier discussion concerning Redfield's modification of his original model of rural society touched on some of the characteristics. The best example of a rural 'farmer' society are the commercial farmers of the United States.

68. Banton comments on a similar pattern of political organization which occurs in the capital of Sierre Leone, Freetown. See Michael Banton, *West African City: A Study of Tribal Life in Freetown*, Oxford, 1957

69. Kingsley Davis and Hilda Hertz Golden, 'Urbanization and Development of Preindustrial Areas' in Paul K. Hatt, and Albert J. Reiss (eds.), *Cities and Society*, Glencoe, Illinois, 1959, pp. 120–40

70. Janet Abu-Lughod, 1961, op. cit., p. 23

71. Doris G. Phillips, 'Rural-To-Urban Migration in Iraq', *Economic Development and Cultural Change*, 7, 4, July, 1959, p. 413

72. H. J. Heeren, 'The Urbanization of Djakarta', *Ekonomi dan Keuangan Indonesia*, 8, 11, November, 1955, 702

73. Donald J. Bogue and K. C. Zachariah, 'Urbanization and Migration in India' in Roy Turner (ed.), *India's Urban Future*, Berkeley, 1961, p. 29

74. Ibid., p. 31

75. Ibid., p. 45

76. Philip M. Hauser (ed.), *Urbanization in Latin America*, New York, 1961, p. 31

77. See U.N.E.S.C.O., *Social Implications of Industrialization and Urbanization in Africa, South of the Sahara*, Paris, 1956

78. See Daniel Lerner, *The Passing of Traditional Society*, Glencoe, Illinois, 1958

79. Kingsley Davis and H. H. Golden, 1959, op. cit., p. 135

80. Robert Redfield, *Peasant Society and Culture*, 1961, p. 77

81. Donald J. Bogue, and K. C. Zachariah, op. cit., p. 53

82. Thomas Hodgkin, op. cit., p. 64

83. William Petersen, 'A General Typology of Migration', *American Sociological Review*, 23, 3, June, 1958, p. 258

84. Little research has as yet been carried out into the psychological attractions which the cities offer to rural migrants. Too often rural-urban migration is analysed in terms of the 'push' factors and the 'pull' factors are not sufficiently investigated. There is a need to understand what kind of images rural people in the non-Western countries have of their cities.

85. See Michael Banton, *The Coloured Quarter–Negro Immigrants in an English City*, London, 1955. Banton makes this point strongly when he is explaining the patterns of assimilation of coloured people in English cities. In contrast to the West Indians, he says, 'The Pakistanis and

Sikhs are examples of non-assimilating or accommodating, as opposed to adapting groups' (p. 75)

86. See E. W. Burgess, 'Accommodation', *Encyclopedia of Social Sciences*, 1, Chicago, 1930, pp. 403–4. Accommodation is defined as '. . . the process of making social adjustments to conflict situations by maintaining social distances between groups and persons which might otherwise come into conflict. . . .'

87. See Philip Mayer, *Townsmen or Tribesmen*, Oxford, 1961

88. There is an additional problem of assessing how the feedback of urban values, etc., is incorporated into the rural society and of trying to build this into the models of rural society.

89. Irene Taeuber, *The Population of Japan*, Princeton, 1958, p. 150

90. This is hardly surprising in a country such as the United States which is highly urbanized. Much of the movement from rural areas to the cities is now made up of Negro and Puerto Rican migration.

91. See Bert F. Hoselitz, 'Urbanization in India', *Kyklos*, XIII, 3, 1960, pp. 361–70

92. The figure of 40 per cent is purely arbitrary and empirical research might suggest a lower or a higher figure. The reason for selecting migrants over 10 years of age is perhaps less obvious. Migrants who do move to urban areas tend to be concentrated in the most fertile age groups, between 15 and 30 years, and the fact that such migration is sometimes sex selective, operates against high birth rates, although in the non-western countries family migration often occurs, and the large number of births in the group of immigrants tend to weight the city-born population unrealistically.

☆ 3 ☆

Revolutionary Change and the Third World City: A Theory of Urban Involution*

One feature of virtually all modernizing nations is the growth of political demands as mass participation increases. The modernization process, by increasing education, mass communications and urbanization creates conditions for mass political participation. Indeed, it is now commonly argued by most students of modernization that political protest, violence and extremist political behaviour typically accompany modernization. Discontent is often great not because a society is stagnant, but because it is changing.[1]

TWO UNDENIABLE facts characterize the majority of the countries of the Third World.[2] First, in the last decade their cities have been growing massively; secondly, this city growth has not been associated with a rate of economic growth which is fast enough to provide employment opportunities for the rapidly increasing populations of these cities.[3] In the face of this situation, the frequently reported outbursts of sporadic violence and rioting are hardly surprising.[4] What is inexplicable is that given a situation in which many of these city populations continue to exist at what appear to be submarginal levels of existence—under conditions of chronic unemployment and underemployment; faced by physical problems of overcrowding and inadequate housing, and continually reminded of their subhuman condition by the affluence of the only too observable city elites—that they have not yet

* This paper was jointly written with Dr. W. R. Armstrong of the Department of Geography, Victoria University of Wellington. I am grateful for his permission to reproduce it in this volume.

proved the base for a successful and genuine revolutionary movement.[5]

It is the purpose of this paper to examine some of the reasons for this lack of revolutionary activity in the larger cities of the underdeveloped world. In the first part of the paper, we put forward a static model of the Third World city economic structure which partly explains how the persistence of 'traditional economic systems' in the Third World city acts as an inhibitor of revolutionary change. In the second part of the paper, we set the facts of this model within the dynamic analysis of the penetration of capitalism, attempting to assess what implications this might have to predictions of revolutionary change.[6]

It is our preliminary contention that a basic reason for the slowness of revolutionary change is the persistence of labour-intensive traditional economic systems which, while characterized by low productivity and underemployment, serve a vitally important function (from the point of view of maintaining the social and political status quo) of providing a 'sense of employment' to many Third World city populations. These labour intensive activities occur primarily in the tertiary or service sectors which form such a large proportion of the Third World cities' occupations.[7] It is therefore necessary to clarify the meaning and the role of this sector in the economic structure of the Third World cities.

A PRELIMINARY DEFINITION OF THE TERTIARY SECTOR[8]

While there has been a considerable debate among Western economists, a broad consensus appears to have been reached on the subject of the definition of 'tertiary occupations', defined by Lampard[9] as the 'activities producing a non-material output'. Most of these authorities agree that these activities have proliferated as a result of the increased technological productivity of the agricultural and manfuacturing sectors which 'allowed a growing proportion of the labour force to be freed to engage in tertiary occupations'. In a passage which has considerable relevance to the Third World, Lampard makes the following significant point about the industrial revolution in Europe:

But if some such transfer of workers into the tertiary area had not occurred in the past, the worst prophecies of the early machine-breakers might have been fulfilled. The numbers of technologically-displaced persons would soon have hobbled labor-saving innovation and lessened the desirability of 'progress'. That our society has never been wholly disenchanted with 'progress' is due, in large part, to the proliferation of tertiary employments. The shift from agriculture and manufacturing has no doubt been painful for those caught in times of rapid techno-organizational change, but the great increases in wealth accruing to communities from their enhanced productive capacity has provided both a cushion and a rationale for the change. It is precisely this prospect of greater productivity which draws people of underdeveloped areas towards the industrial revolution. One hopes that the social costs of industrialization will not prove a rude awakening.[10]

The evidence for this pattern being repeated in the underdeveloped societies is not strong,[11] and one is inclined to wonder in societies where technological-displacement is a sectorally-imbalanced phenomenon—that is, it is occurring in manufacturing, but not in agricultural, sectors—why many of these societies do not become 'disenchanted' with progress, at least in the Western model, and revert to some other kind of model for development. Indeed, one can find the more intelligent of the economic planners advocating forms of investment that would avoid labour redundancy. Thus such people advocate 'intermediate' technology and investment in agriculture which aims largely at increasing productivity through the use of better seeds, pesticides, etc., thus avoiding the problem of unemployment and underemployment.[12] But in most societies of the Third World, a gap still remains between the logic of such advocacy and the ability to put these plans into practice.

The reasons for this vary from society to society. In some societies the planners and politicians have been so moulded and influenced by the Western model of the industrial revolution that they are incapable of rethinking the problems of development within the unique conditions of their own society. One might add that the problem can apply equally to the socialist societies as well as those within the capitalist framework. In

66

other societies, problems of economic development have barely been touched because of the pressure on the political elites to establish custody of their newly-independent nation states. There are two reasons why this rethinking of economic policy has not occurred. First, and most significant, is the fact that the majority of the Third World societies have emerged as independent nations embedded in a system of international capitalism. Paul Baran and Gundar Frank[13] argue effectively that it is the subordinate position of the Third World nations within this system of international capitalism which is the fundamental reason for their fumbling efforts at economic development. But to this fact must be added the important variable of population, for the majority of these societies, such as India, are undergoing rapid population increase. We do not intend here to adopt a Malthusian position for, after all, the experience of the Western European countries and, indeed, of the United States is one of exceptionally rapid population growth after industrial takeoff and during the periods of their most rapid economic growth. However, when such population growth in the underdeveloped countries is associated with a failure to reform the structure of the country in such a way as to utilize the available labour—a failure which primarily stems from the interlocking nature of international capitalism— population growth simply becomes a drag on investment. This situation we can see only too clearly in the context of societies such as India and Indonesia. Despite the pessimism of these comments, is there any reason to believe that such situations inherently will bring about conditions which will precipitate radical change in the immediate future in these countries?

We believe not, and the reason for our viewpoint stems from a pragmatic investigation of the economic structure of the Third World city and its relationships with its rural hinterland and international capitalism. It is only by setting the tertiary sector within the total city's economic structure that one can understand its extremely complex nature and its characteristics. One might add at this point that the problems of defining the tertiary sector on the basis of employment in the Third World context are exceptionally difficult. The most ambitious attempt has been made by Maunder[14] in his study of Kingston,

Jamaica. Even this excellent attempt to come to terms with the problem fails because of the theoretical misunderstanding of the structure of the city's economy. Until adequate statistics are collected on the basis of a revised conceptual understanding of the economic structure, it is impossible to arrive at truly accurate estimates of employment in this sector. In this paper no attempt is made to define 'tertiary sector' rigorously. We consider the characteristics adequately explained as seen in the total economic structure of the Third World city.

THE ECONOMIC STRUCTURE
OF THE THIRD WORLD CITY

In describing the economic structure of the Third World city, we have drawn extensively on Geertz'[15] analysis of Modjokuto, an anonymously named town in Java, Indonesia. It may be that in utilizing an Indonesian town as the basis for a generalization on the economic structure of a Third World city, we are utilizing an aberrant example which is not applicable in other underdeveloped countries. Of course, a great deal depends upon what may be labelled as the 'economic base' of the town under discussion. In some cases there may be towns in underdeveloped countries, generally single-function centred; such as oil towns, which are totally within the orbit of a capitalist-centred economy. In other cases, there may be different functioning centres, such as Kudus, described by Castles[16] where the economic base of the town is almost totally concerned with the manufacture of cigarettes, but the town lies almost entirely within the labour-intensive sector. Despite these differences, our argument is that the majority of towns in the Third World, particularly the large primate cities, have an economic structure similar to that described by Geertz.[17]

In Modjokuto, Geertz[18] points out that the economic structure of the town is divided into two parts—a firm-centred economy 'where trade and industry occur through a set of impersonally-defined social institutions which organize a variety of specialized occupations with respect to some particular productive or distributive ends'. The second part is made up of the bazaar economy which is based on 'the independent activities of a set of highly competitive commodity traders who

68

relate to one another, mainly by means of an incredible volume of ad hoc acts of exchange'.[19]

On the face of it, this distinction between the two sectors of this city's economy might be said to approximate the model of the dual economy.[20] Certainly it has affinities with the model of technological and economic dualism put forward by Higgins[21] to the extent that the firm-centred economy is clearly capital-intensive and the bazaar economy is labour-intensive, utilizing very different types of technology and capital. But it must be made clear that the acceptance of such a viewpoint does not inhibit the view of the city's economy as a whole,[22] for these two sectors do not fall into distinct boxes: indeed they are interlaced. The manufacture and flow of goods and services which are both created and passed through the city, are generated in each of the sectors. Figure 3 shows the kind of pattern which such goods and services take.[23] This diagram makes it clear that employment in the tertiary sector would originate in both the bazaar and the firm-centred economic sectors. There are, of course, certain employment categories which are difficult to place within one or the other of these two sectors. Most obvious is the problem of placing government employees, most of whom are employed in 'service' industries. In some countries, most government employment could usefully be fitted into the firm-centred sector, but in general, if one looks at the patterns of government employment in underdeveloped countries, one is more inclined to say that the patterns of bureaucracy tend towards labour-intensive practices which are essentially a reflection of the bazaar-economy principles. Excellent examples can be found in Indonesia, India and the Philippines. Despite such difficulties of classification, the most obvious difference between the two sectors is in terms of the 'quantity' of employment they can offer. In the capital-intensive sector, where productivity is high, the possibilities for employment are limited by labour-destroying innovations; on the other hand, in the bazaar-type economy, the possibilities for employment are much greater even though returns are much smaller and the end-product of this situation is frequently what Wertheim[24] has called a condition of 'shared poverty', and Breese,[25] less satisfactorily, 'subsistence urbanization'.

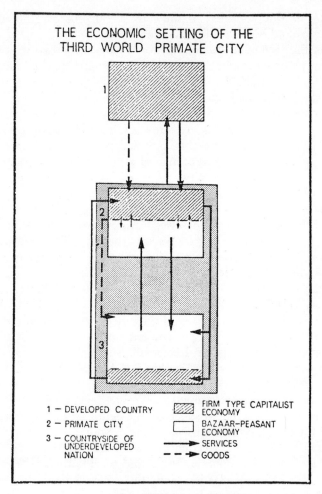

Figure 3

Finally, one may be critical of the model of these two sectors in that it presents too simple a division; for instance, there appears to be, particularly amongst immigrant groups in Third World cities and the countryside, forms of economic organization which combine, in an intermediate fashion, elements of both the firm-type economy and the bazaar

70

economy.[26] Despite these suggested limitations, it is our argument that they do not invalidate the model used. Indeed, an understanding of the role and characteristics of the tertiary sector in the Third World city does aid in the critical evaluation of some predictive models of social and economic change which have been developed by Western theorists; which we shall analyse later. At this point, it is possible to consider, in the light of the model elaborated, the critical question of the role which the tertiary sector in the Third World city can play in creating employment opportunities for the city's population.

THE ROLE OF THE TERTIARY SECTOR

The first point to clarify with respect to the question of the provision of employment opportunities, is the supposed employment limits of the tertiary sector, for it is in the finite qualities of the employment in this sector that the major dangers for the stability of the city economies and political structures are said to exist. If one accepts, following Maunder,[27] that there are only three categories into which the employable may fall—employed, underemployed, and non-employed—then one has to ask the question: Do the same concepts which lead to the formulation of these categories operate in both sectors of the Third World city economic structure? On the face of it, one must say 'Yes', for there are only, it would appear, two types of employment—full-time and part-time. But, with respect to the forms of underemployment, there is a wide range of possibilities; indeed we would suggest some distinction between the types of unemployment in the firm-type sector and those in the bazaar economy. First, it would appear that underemployment defined as 'a situation in which there are many more people employed than is necessary on a "rational" basis'[28] is far more common in the bazaar sector than in the firm-type economy. On the other hand unemployment defined as a condition in which labour is actively seeking work, but unemployed full-time, is far more common in the firm-type structure. This is not to argue that the two types of unemployment are exclusively confined to 'sectors', but simply to say that the majority of cases of each type occur in them.[29]

Broadly speaking then, it can be argued that there are

different patterns of unemployment and underemployment, as well as of employment operating in the two economic sectors elaborated. If this is the case, we can now extend this argument to investigate the role the tertiary sector plays in absorbing labour within the city structure. It should be clear by now that it is the bazaar economy which is the most absorptive.

The question is, 'Why?'. Geertz'[30] description of the economic characteristics of the bazaar economy of the Indonesian town of Modjokuto provides some of the answer. It is quite clear that he is referring to the total bazaar economy including the production and sales sectors as part of 'one comprehensive, economic institution'.[31] Central to this system is the market or *pasar* which is the focus and centre of the trading patterns which permeate the whole hinterland of the town. But as Geertz[32] points out, the terms can be applied in a much broader sense:

> Thus by the pasar we mean not simply that particular square eighth of a mile o˙ so of sheds and platforms, set apart in the center of the town, where (as someone has said of the classical emporium) men are permitted each day to deceive one another, but the whole pattern of small-scale peddling and processing activity characteristic of the Modjokuto area generally.

The understanding of the system rests on a knowledge of three of its aspects: (i) the flow of goods and services, (ii) the set of economic mechanisms which sustains and regulates the flow of goods and services, and (iii) the socio-cultural role of the *pasar* system.

From the point of view of the first of these aspects—the flow of goods and services—Geertz indicates that the most important characteristic is the type of goods which flow through the market. In general, the small, easily transportable, storable products allow a flow through the market which tends to move in circles, passing from traders over an extended period. As Geertz[33] says:

> Like Javanese agriculture, Javanese trading is highly labor intensive; and perhaps the best, if slightly caricatured image for it is that of a long line of men passing bricks from hand to

hand over some greatly extended distance to build, slowly and brick by brick, a large wall.

The regulatory mechanisms which control this system include a sliding price system, a complex balance of carefully-managed credit relationship, and an extensive fractionalization of risks as a corollary of profit margins. These regulatory mechanisms tend to have the effect of fractionalizing the trading activity thus allowing the introduction of more individuals into the system. Finally, there is a socio-cultural role of the bazaar system. Here Geertz[34] stresses that the *pasar* system operates in an impersonal manner; for instance, he comments:

A man and his brother, a son and his father, even a wife and her husband will commonly operate on their own at the bazaar and regard one another within that context with nearly as cold an eye as they would any other trader.

This statement is important for it would appear to indicate that total labour commitment within the economic unit of the family,[35] is not operating in the system. Belshaw[36] is critical of Geertz' viewpoint, arguing that:

There is no such thing as an enduring non-personalistic relationship, and no economy in the world can be based entirely or even largely on non-personalistic relationships for this would be the negation of continuity and security and would be atomistic group behaviour rather than behaviour in a society.

It would seem that he is being less than fair to Geertz because the latter does admit that what he calls 'particularistic relationships' do exist in the market place, although he argues concretely that they are not the most significant relationship. There appears to be some confusion over the question of the actual labour and the institutional organization which appropriates the profits of the labour. While the members of a family may compete in the market places, this does not conflict with the taking of the profits by the head of the household. Thus, as Geertz points out, a man who wishes to introduce his son to the *pasar* trading system will not always take him out as an apprentice, but simply give him goods on credit and let him peddle them as best he can. In our opinion, this does not, however, negate the principle of total labour commitment. By the provision of goods the household head presumably accepts this principle. These then are the major aspects of the bazaar economy. It is now possible to summarize the major reasons why it can absorb increasing labour—or, to borrow yet another term from the fertile imagination of Geertz,[37] why the *pasar* sector has the capacity to 'involute'. In attempting to explain the extraordinary capacity of the peasant agriculture of Java to absorb increasing labour as population grows, Geertz has emphasized the significant role of wet-rice cultivation which seems to allow marginal levels of labour productivity to be maintained despite the working-in of additional labour. Four features characterize the process of involution: (i) a tenacity of basic pattern; (ii) internal elaboration and ornateness; (iii) technical hair-splitting; and (iv) unending virtuosity.

All these characteristics occur within the bazaar sector of the Third World city structure which has the capacity to undergo a similar process of involution despite its radically different ecological base. What are the reasons for this? First, the institutional basis of the enterprise in the bazaar economy is still the family, even though members of the family may operate independently in the market-place, and the major labour commitment is still total; thus the head-of-the-house is committed to ensuring members of his family entrance into this system. Secondly, the systems of flow of goods and services which characterize the bazaar system allow the introduction of more labour. Thirdly, the bazaar system has something of a self-inflationary quality. Thus the more people who enter the system, the greater the market. The simplest example is the proliferation of prepared-food vendors whose numbers increase as the population of the cities increases.[38] The fourth factor is the relationship of the bazaar sector to the peasant economy. The population movement and the flow of goods and services between the two sectors is common, thus allowing greater flexibility both in terms of seasonal labour and longer-term employment. Finally there is the relationship of the bazaar sector to the capital-intensive sector. Here the siphoning downwards of the greater profits earned in the latter sector, whether it be in wages for servants, or in employment on construction of prestige projects, or in forms of welfare, enables the bazaar sector to absorb greater population.

These, then, are the major features of the bazaar economy and its relationship with the other sectors of a country's economy, which enables it to absorb labour. We can now turn to the last of our questions and consider the implications of this analysis for the problems of the future of economic growth and revolutionary change in the Third World countries.

THE IMPLICATIONS OF 'URBAN INVOLUTIONS' FOR MODELS OF ECONOMIC AND POLITICAL GROWTH AND REVOLUTIONARY CHANGE

We have looked so far at the tertiary sector of the Third World city and at the role it plays, and we have set out the implications of the answers to these two questions for the problems of economic development and employment in underdeveloped countries. Having reached these conclusions, our intention now is to set them against the predictive models of a number of Western-centred theorists in an endeavour to establish the validity and reality of opposing viewpoints.

For most Western social scientists, the emergence of the service sector to a position of importance, even dominance, in the highly-developed industrial nations has been accepted as an integral and natural evolution of these economies. Not only does the service sector provide a significant part of urban employment; it is frequently the largest single employer of labour in the whole economy.

It has been shown that this high proportion of tertiary employment is positively correlated with a high level of urbanization and a considerable degree of economic development.[39] It seems logical that in countries with such high levels of urbanization most of the tertiary employment will be concentrated in cities, if only because most of the population is located there. Lampard,[40] for instance, argues that, 'the city is the only feasible locus for the mass of specialized servicing ... in that ... its product is closely tied to the consuming population which is overwhelmingly urban or suburban'. The market, of

75

course, is only one of the attractions for servicing industries; the whole range of attractions associated with the external economies provided by cities exert at least as strong a pull for servicing activity as it does for manufacturing. The proposition is not universally exclusive, however. In some countries which rely heavily on tourism much of the tertiary employment is located in semi-rural areas where tourists attempt to escape the overcrowded metropolitan areas of the rest of Europe, and indeed, of the United States. Such examples are usually exceptions to the general rule. In fact, the continued concentration of service industry in the cities of the economically advanced countries has been attacked on the grounds that it is not in the interests of social or regional balance in a society.[41] But most empirical evidence in developed capitalist societies certainly supports the assertion[42] that the high proportion of tertiary employment in the capitalist city can be regarded as a sign of economic growth, if not social well-being.

In the context of the Third World countries, similar high levels of tertiary employment in their cities have not always been regarded in the same favourable light. One writer has argued that this 'gross inflation of the tertiary sector'[43] will have disastrous repercussions on the stability of the society largely because it leads to the creation of an 'impoverished and explosive lumpen-proletariat'.[44] The concentration of such a group in the cities, argues Tangri,[45] provides a politically-malleable and revolutionary-oriented population. The most vigorous exposition of the revolutionary potential of this group has been outlined by Fanon[46] who sees the lumpen-proletariat as forming a significant element in the eventual overthrow of the existing governments. 'The constitution of a lumpen-proletariat is a phenomenon which obeys its own logic, and neither the brimming activity of the missionaries nor the decrees of the central government can check its growth. This lumpen-proletariat is like a horde of rats; you may kick them, throw stones at them, but despite your efforts, they will go on boring at the roots of the tree.'[47] Other writers have criticized the proliferation of the tertiary sectors of the Third World cities on economic grounds, arguing that the growth of this sector is both unproductive and economically irrational.[48] André

Gundar Frank[49] sums up this attitude when he describes the proliferation of workers in the tertiary sector of Chilean cities in the following terms:

Far from being a mark of development, as a reading of Sir William Petty and Colin Clark might once have led us to believe, this structure and distribution are a reflection of Chile's structural underdevelopment: 60 per cent of the employed, not to speak of the unemployed and under-employed, work in activities that do not produce goods—in a society that obviously in a high degree lacks goods.

But opposing viewpoints have been put forth by other writers who have argued that this growth of tertiary services in the cities is an understandable, indeed a necessary, phenomenon. For instance, Ginsburg[50] has pointed out that the concentration of services is a reflection of the basic rural structure of most of the underdeveloped societies where there are '. . . only a limited number of services performed by the cities'. Other writers, such as Morse, argue that the excessive numbers employed within the service sector may not have unhappy repercussions. He goes on to say, 'The question occurs, do not people generally seek out the most advantageous employment, and would not those who are in "petty services" tend to be less productive in the other occupations open to them? May not Latin American city growth be reallocating the working force into more effective occupational patterns?'[51] This kind of reasoning raises more questions than it answers—do people seek out their most advantageous employment in a labour-surplus situation or do they take what is offering? What is a more effective occupational pattern? More effective to whom? The employer, the employee, the nation's economy?[52] Yet another writer has indicated that the tertiary sector has the function of a 'residual employer' taking up the slack from other sectors at times of economic stagnation. Its capacity is aided by the 'low investment necessary for the initiation of the activities. Neither complex physical plants nor prolonged periods of education and training need to be undertaken in many of the service and commerce occupations'.[53] If the views of the latter group of writers are accepted, then it may be possible to agree with the economist Hirschman's[54] position which would regard this 'infiltration' of

77

tertiary services as a necessary imbalancing part of the processes of economic growth. His argument based on the proposition of unbalanced growth and the execution of bottlenecks is as follows: As part of the process of economic growth within what one would label the capitalist-penetrated structure at certain stages of economic growth, the opportunities for employment in the 'capital-intensive' industries do not increase at a fast enough rate despite overall increases in productivity in this sector. The surplus labour is thus absorbed into the small-scale industry in the tertiary sector where wages are low and only small capital investment is needed. This situation, however, is only temporary, for the growth of the 'capital-intensive' sector is eventually sufficient to iron out the unbalancing effects of retardation in the tertiary and agricultural sectors of the economy. There is some evidence for this pattern occurring in the case of Japan.[55] Sir Arthur Lewis[56] is less optimistic. He points out that although Karl Marx' belief 'that in the capitalist system employment-destroying innovations would always be excessive relative to employment-creating innovations, and he therefore predicted an ever-growing army of unemployed', may not be true for the advanced countries of Western Europe, the statement may prove to be correct in the context of the underdeveloped societies of the contemporary world. A 'capital-intensive' development based on imported plant is forced on the countries of the underdeveloped world because of their technological lag and their distorted price structures. The result, says Lewis, is that despite industrial development, unemployment increases. While not stating it specifically, he infers that such a situation may be disastrous for the stability and future of these countries. One further view-point of the tertiary sectors of these cities needs to be recorded. Some writers, for instance Keyfitz,[57] have pointed out that at least employment in the tertiary sector, even if it is not full employment, fulfils the function of 'quieting the claims of those who would otherwise be left out of the division of wealth', thus at least proving to be politically stabilizing, if not always economically rational.

In summary then, one can broadly divide these views about the roles and character of the tertiary sector in the under-

78

developed country into two groups: first, those writers who
regard the present inflated tertiary sector of the Third World
cities as indications of the failure of a particular form of
economic development and as inbuilt danger points for the
future of the present political and economic systems of those
societies; and, secondly, those writers who regard the present
unstable situation as one which will eventually be corrected
with overall economic growth. It is possible to illustrate the
predictive characteristics of these models by the use of dia-
grams. Figure 4 indicates the first school of thought. In this

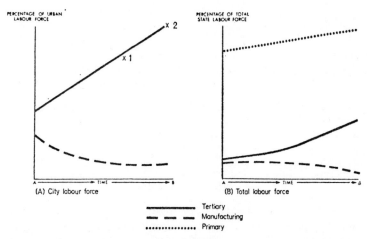

Figure 4. Future distribution of labour force by occupational sectors.
Predictive Model A

diagram, the changes which the city employment structures
will undergo are illustrated. It assumes an overall condition of
economic equilibrium in a society which affects both the
agricultural and the urban sectors. The inability of the agricultural sector to absorb increasing labour forces this labour
into the towns, but employment is not available in manufacturing; consequently, it flows into the tertiary sector. At point
X^2 (arbitrarily chosen) there is a condition of unemployment,
and finally the lack of employment creates the explosive revolutionary characteristics in the lumpen-proletariat which enables

79

it to overthrow the existing entrenched forces. Figure 5 represents the other school of thought which sees this inflation of the service sector as purely a temporary phenomenon, and the lack of employment in manufacturing as a phenomenon which will be ironed out with increasing productivity and wealth in the society. At the same time, the population in the agricultural sector will decline and overall urbanization in the society will increase.

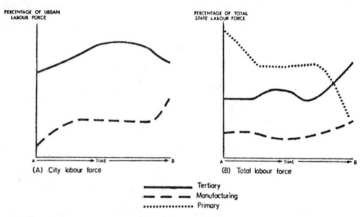

Figure 5. Future distribution of labour force by occupational sectors. Predictive Model B

Despite the wide disparity in their analysis and conclusions, both groups have one facet in common—they regard employment in the tertiary sector of the city economy as finite. The sector is capable of absorbing only so much labour at a particular stage of economic development; after that labour will become underemployed, unemployed or will be forced into some other sector of the economy. It is the writers' assertion that this view stems to a large extent from what we may label a Western-centric[58] viewpoint which regards the tertiary sector as related to the level of economic development, despite the very obvious fact that this is not the case in the majority of countries which they are investigating. In other words, all these writers have certain built-in preconceptions about the form, function and role of the tertiary sector which they have formulated on the basis of studies in the developed world which are not applicable in every sense to many underdeveloped economies. It is because of these Western-centred preconceptions that the predictive capacities, based on such arguments, may be invalidated. We argue, therefore, that the actual characteristics of the tertiary sector in each underdeveloped country should be closely studied and evaluated before predictive models are attempted. In advocating this, we are aware that the model established in this paper is neither unique nor unchanging. In setting out a case study of a traditional system of an urban *pasar*-peasant agricultural sector—a traditional sector which has a labour-absorbing function which slows or deflects the emergence of a revolutionary explosion for a time (existing alongside the modern capitalist sector)—we realize that other situations exist or may develop in other Third World countries.

In the first place, a change in the structure of the urban-bazaar system itself could take place if the capitalist sector found it worthwhile participating in the economic activities of the bazaar—on its own terms and using its own methods, of course. The significant aspect of this change is not just that the commercial and organizational activities of the bazaar system are penetrated, but that the attitudes of those in the sector are permeated as a result of such penetration. This cracking of the cultural insulation is perhaps the most significant and devastating breach of the dividing line between the capital-intensive enclave and the traditional sector.

Geertz[59] discusses the process of transformation of Modjokuto's 'would-be entrepreneurial class'[60] as the town's social structure transforms 'from a composite of self-contained and socially-segregated status groups to a more broadly comprehensive set of across-the-board social classes. At the top of this hesitantly emerging class system are the leaders of the various political and quasi-political *aliran* organizations; at the bottom the steadily expanding urban proletariat'.[61] And as these attitudes change, a concomitant change takes place in the commercial forms and institutions of exchange:

This intimate relationship between a well-administered business community and a modernized urban social structure is, in fact, fairly clearly recognized, at least on the commercial side, by the people of Modjokuto town themselves. 'They too . . . distinguish between the pasar trading complex and the toko store complex, and they do so mainly in terms of contrast between "modern" (*moderen*) and "old-fashioned" (*kolot*).'[62]

It can be assumed that the gradual change from *pasar* to *toko* forms of trading will bring in its train considerable changes in organization. The most crucial of these will be:

(a) the growth of larger scale operations;
(b) a greater concentration of capital in the hands of the *toko* entrepreneur;
(c) the reluctance of the new-style entrepreneur to spread his business widely among his fellow traders—as is typical of the *pasar* system. This is then associated with an increased willingness to take greater risks for larger returns which in turn will be ploughed partially into organizational or technological innovation;
(d) a reduction in the flow of goods in 'hundreds of little trickles, funnelled through an enormous number of transactions',[63] which characterize the absorptive *pasar* system; and so, finally;
(e) a decline in labour input and a tightening rein placed on the capacity of the dwindling *pasar* system to absorb labour and keep an underemployed (in Western terms) urban work force at an acceptable, if subsistence, standard of living.

It cannot be emphasized too much that the effectiveness of this form of capitalist penetration of the traditional sector lies not only in the influence it has on the methods of carrying out urban economic activity. More invidious for the 'old-fashioned' structure is the way it changes attitudes and creates a new and expanding range of felt needs—for shoes, bicycles, manufactured furniture, ready-made clothing and so on—as Geertz himself points out. All these wants, as he says, are 'directly adjusted to the Western-influenced revolution in tastes which the emerging urban classes are experiencing'.[64]

In the Third World, then, Geertz argues, economic development is tending to take a classical Weberian form, 'a gener-

ally disesteemed group of small shopkeepers and petty manu-
facturers arising out of a traditional trading class is attempting
to secure an improved status in a changing society'.[65] The
emergence of this group means that there is now the prototype
of a Western-type of petty commercial (and, to a much smaller
extent, industrial) capitalist in Third World cities. But of even
greater significance, the very existence of this group not only
leads to the reduction of traditional modes of production and
exchange; it also facilitates the subversion of the *pasar* system
and the takeover of much of its activity by the large-scale
enterprises in the capital-intensive sector.

In acknowledging that this process is occurring in many cities
of the Third World, and has proceeded so far in some that the
bazaar structure has been largely destroyed, the writers wish
to emphasize that there is still a majority of cities in which the
pasar system is dominant, and in which such direct capitalist
penetration has not proceeded far. Nevertheless, the stand taken
by the first group of theorists may in the longer term be valid
and their Western-centric point of view become more relevant
as the cities of the Third World become increasingly penetrated
and Westernized. Further strength is given to their case—again
in the longer term—if we take into account another process of
capitalist penetration which has been occurring in countries of
the Third World.

As we stated earlier, the traditional system of economic
activity consists of an interlocking urban-bazaar, rural-peasant
agricultural structure in which the former depends to a considerable degree for its food supplies on the latter. In turn, the
urban sector funnels non-agricultural supplies to the peasant
sector, as well as absorbing those who migrate from the rural
areas. The function of the urban tertiary sector as a safety valve
is therefore heavily dependent on the close ties it has with the
peasant sector. Consequently, its capacity to absorb labour
and to act as a cushion against urban and rural discontent
depends to an important extent on the continued existence of
its peasant–agricultural resource base.

This raises a highly significant question. What happens
when, as in some Caribbean countries, the capitalist system
effectively penetrates the whole economy? In examples such as

pre-revolutionary Cuba and contemporary Puerto Rico, it is no longer possible to talk in terms of a dual society, in the definition outlined earlier, because capitalist penetration has been so comprehensive that the areas left outside the commercialized, market economy are minute. Here the rural sector has been as thoroughly commercialized as the urban. By the early decades of this century, the agricultural sectors of both countries had been predominantly geared to capital-intensive cash-crop production in the company estates which also controlled the commercial crop-growing peasants producing for the sugar *centrales*—the companies' 'factories in the field'.

In circumstances such as these there is likely to be little surplus in the way of food or handicraft products to support the bazaar systems in the cities. The subverting of the peasant system therefore has much wider effects than in the rural area. It is likely to cause a breakdown of the entire rural–urban traditional structure by limiting drastically the volume of produce exchanged in the bazaar, and perhaps even hastens the advent of discontent by throwing dispossessed peasants into cities in which there are few outlets for bazaar-type subsistence economic activity.[66]

Cuba is the extreme case of this process. By the end of the 1950s, the entire economy had become an almost classical Marxist example of a nineteenth-century capitalist entity with class polarization in the cities and the rural areas—and there was little easing of the disparities between the classes in either. In this milieu there were few outlets to absorb disaffection or to satisfy felt needs. Because the nation was so permeated—economically, socially, culturally—by Western capitalism, and because no indigenous urban–rural involution was possible, the ideal situation for social revolution was reached.[67]

Other countries, especially in Latin-America, are showing similar symptoms though not as acute yet as in Cuba. Some countries such as Puerto Rico and Jamaica have had a safety valve provided by labour absorption through external migration (though this is drastically reduced in Jamaica now). But in most countries of Latin-America, the penetrative process is continuing.

Two conclusions arise out of this. The first is that the traditional urban service sector is heavily dependent upon the existence of a traditional rural productive base. When (and if) that base is penetrated and largely replaced by another system of production, the urban bazaar, lacking a course of supply for a great part of its activity, is weakened if not destroyed as an indigenous involuted system. The second conclusion follows from this: the growth of—or even the continued existence of— the urban bazaar system in the Third World city is not a self-contained process. It is ultimately dependent upon the activities and policies of the capitalist sector. Under conditions of continued penetration of the traditional structure—whether in the city or the countryside—by capitalist modes of production and/or appropriation, traditional labour absorptive capacity would fall and the polarization between the modern capital-intensive sector and the unemployed urban lumpen-proletariat would come out into the open.

If we express the above discussion of capitalist expansionary movement in diagrammatic form, we have a diagram showing the roles played in the economy of an underdeveloped country by the capitalist and traditional systems. Figure 6 shows the gradual expansion of the capital-intensive system into the agricultural, manufacturing and service sectors of the economy, and the consequent increase in the proportion contributed by it to G.N.P. (Or, to put the emphasis on the more important part of the process, the proportion of G.N.P. appropriated by the capital-intensive sector.)

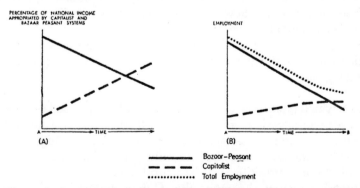

Figure 6. Output and employment in capitalist and bazaar–peasant systems in underdeveloped countries

This diagram also illustrates the result in terms of employment. As the capital-intensive forms of production move into agriculture, larger scale, more mechanized techniques drive labour from the land. Here, as in other sectors, labour inputs axiomatically are reduced. Even where peasants are left on the land, less labour is usually required for commercial cropping, except for some crops at seasonal peak periods.

With its product supply base reduced, the bazaar sector's activities decrease. At the same time, landless peasants pour into the cities looking for work, which neither the capitalist nor weakened bazaar sectors can provide in sufficient quantity. This process has been expressed visually in Figure 7 which is basically the same as Figure 3, but with 'change' built in to take account of the gradual transformation of the indigenous economy from traditional to capitalist modes of production.

CONCLUSION

The latter part of this discussion should not be seen as a contradiction of the original proposition of the article. Rather, it has been an attempt to see the processes of change operating in the economies of underdeveloped countries over a time span. To fall back on the diagrammatic illustrations, we have taken the original Figure 3 of an underdeveloped economy with its traditional sectors and the capitalist enclave operating side by side. We have then injected the dynamic of capitalist expansion into the model to allow us to determine what the likely results of this process might be. We have come to the conclusion that, in the long term, the predictions of the first group of writers are likely to have the greater validity because of the type of change taking place.

But this does not in any way invalidate the original proposition which establishes the model of an underdeveloped economy at a certain period of time. Figure 8 illustrates the point by setting out the two static models—one which we might term the 'Indonesian' example with only partial infiltration of the still largely traditional urban/rural sector by the capital-intensive sector; the other the 'Cuban' model in which the penetration has continued to such a degree that almost the

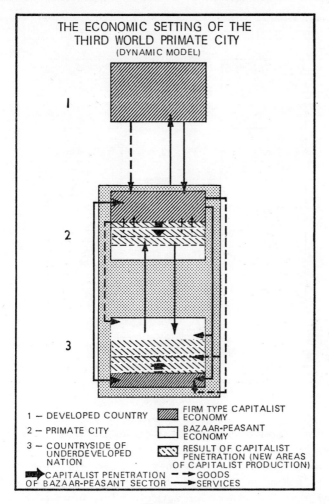

Figure 7

entire economy has been Westernized by the capitalist sector.
These are the two poles. What we have been discussing in the
latter stages of this paper is the process which could lead from
the one to the other.

Of course it is not inevitable that capitalist penetration will
invariably convert the 'Indonesian' model into the 'Cuban'—

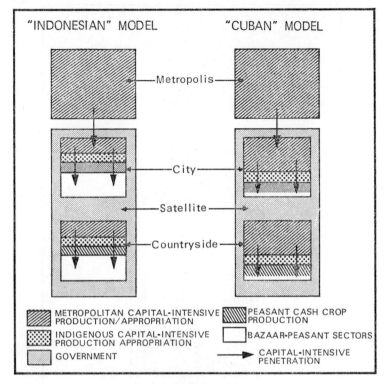

Figure 8

the involution of international capitalism that seems to be emerging with the ever closer commercial contacts among the advanced industrial nations may slow the process, or cause it to be diverted in some way—but recent case studies[68] seem to show that the process of agricultural commercialization is proceeding steadily in certain underdeveloped countries.

In concluding, then, the writers re-emphasize that the proposition established in the first part of this paper has value in its analysis of the urban economic structures of many underdeveloped countries. But of much greater significance are the implications which derive from this analysis concerning the impact of capitalist penetration in the Third World. The results of this penetration are, we argue, far less homogeneous in their effects than the predictive models we have evaluated would have led us to believe, simply because the Third World is not the homogeneous entity they suppose it to be. More precisely, the countries of the Third World are at different stages of development—or under-development—as a result of their varying historical experiences of capitalism, their indigenous socio-economic structures, and the interaction of the one on the other. Although in the long term the first group may be proved correct in its predictions, revolutionary change will not proceed along a broad front in the short or even medium term. Rather, it appears more logical that the revolutionary changes will be delayed longer in countries where the traditional structures are more resilient, and where there are social and economic outlets for the indigenous population, than in countries where these structures have been subverted by capitalist penetration, or where no effective traditional structures ever existed.

NOTES

1. Myron Weiner, 'Urbanisation and Political Protest', *Civilisations*, 1967, Vol. XVII, Nos. 1 and 2, p. 44. It should be made clear that we begin our paper with this quotation not because we agree with it; indeed much of the evidence of this paper invalidates its assertions, but because it represents what may be labelled as the 'conventional wisdom' of the Western social scientists who are attempting to create a rationale for the processes of change occurring in the Third World.

2. Excluding the Communist societies of China, Cuba and North Vietnam, as defined by Peter Worsley, *The Third World*, 1964

3. McGee has labelled this process 'pseudo-urbanization' in another publication. See T. G. McGee, *The Southeast Asian City*, 1967, pp. 15–22

4. For instance see Peter C. W. Gutkind, 'The Energy of Despair: Social Organisations of the Unemployed in two African Cities: Lagos and Nairobi', *Civilisations*, 1967, Vol. XVII, No. 3, pp. 186–214

5. There are, of course, obvious reasons for this lack of success. The physical concentration of population in the city allows theoretically at least easier surveillance and military counteraction. Discontented groups are more easily manipulated for political ends; for example, the student groups in Djakarta. But as the Negroes of the United States and the Tet offensive in South Vietnam illustrate well enough, neither of these reasons has universal validity.

6. It is necessary to point out that we mean 'revolutionary', in the sense of genuine revolutionary change designed to overturn and replace the institutions subordinating the neo-colonial states to international capitalism. It should also be made clear that we use 'traditional' and 'preindustrial' as explanatory terms for economies which are practices

characterized by labour-intensive, low capital investment and comparatively poor technology. The firm-centred economy is equated with capital-intensive economies.

7. Adequate figures on the proportion of tertiary workers in the cities of the Third World are not easily available. For some information the reader is referred to Philip M. Hauser (ed.), *Urbanisation in Latin America*, 1961, p. 120; Roy Turner (ed.), *India's Urban Future*, 1962, p. 166. T. G. McGee, *The Southeast Asian City*, 1967, p. 89, and for a more general coverage see U.N.E.S.C.O., *Social Implications of the Industrialisation and Urbanisation in Africa South of the Sahara*, 1964, pp. 21–3, 26–34. Labour-intensive forms also persist in cottage industry, but this has difficulty persisting in the face of the capital-intensive sector's industrial competition. In some cases cottage industry is surprisingly resilient. See Jacques Dupuis, *Madras et le Nord du Coromandel*, 1960, Chapter IX

8. One of the earlier attempts to define the tertiary sector is that of Colin Clark. See Colin Clark, *The Conditions of Economic Progress*, 1940

9. Eric E. Lampard, 'The History of Cities in Economically Advanced Areas', John Friedmann and William Alonso, *Regional Development and Planning. A Reader*, 1964, p. 340

10. Ibid., p. 340

11. See for instance, S. G. Trantis, 'The Economic Progress, Occupational Distribution and International Terms of Trade', *Economic Journal*, LXIII, 1953, 627–37

12. See Sir Arthur Lewis, 'Unemployment in Developing Countries', *The World Today*, January, 1967, No. 1, pp. 20–1

13. See Paul A. Baran, *The Political Economy of Growth*, 1957, and André Gundar Frank, *Capitalism and Underdevelopment in Latin America*, 1967

14. W. F. Maunder, *Employment in an Underdeveloped Area. A Sample Survey of Kingston, Jamaica*, 1960

15. See Clifford Geertz, *Peddlers and Princes. Social Change and Economic Modernisation in Two Indonesian Towns*, 1963; and *The Social History of an Indonesian Town*, 1965

16. Lance Castles, *Religion, Politics and Economic Behaviour in Java: The Kudus Cigarette Industry*, 1967

17. Another excellent description of the economic structure of the Third World city is that of Jacques Dupuis, op. cit.

18. Geertz (1963), p. 28

19. Ibid., p. 28

20. See J. H. Boeke, *Economics and Economic Policy of Dual Societies*, 1953

21. Benjamin Higgins, 'The "Dualistic Theory" of Underdeveloped Areas', *Economic Development and Cultural Change*, Vol. 4, No. 2, January, 1956

22. In this respect one may be sympathetic with Frank's criticism of the concept of the dual economy, but not take his extreme viewpoint that the concept is totally invalid. See André Gundar Frank, 1967, and 'Sociology of Development and Underdevelopment of Sociology', *Catalyst*, No. 3. Summer 1967, pp. 18–73

23. It is interesting to note that after the construction of this model we found similar models, devoted to particular products, in a study of marketing in Madagascar. G. Donque, 'Le Zoma de Tananarive. Étude géographique d'un marché urbain', *Madagascar, Revue de Geographie*, No. VIII, janvier–juillet, 1966, pp. 93–273

24. W. F. Wertheim, *East–West Parallels: Sociological Approaches to Modern Asia*, 1964, pp. 165–81

25. Gerald Breese, *Urbanisation in Newly Developing Countries*, 1966

26. See G. William Skinner, *Chinese Society in Thailand: An Analytical History*, 1957. For an example in the rural context see D. W. Fryer and J. C. Jackson, 'Chinese Smallholders in Selangor', *Pacific Viewpoint*, September, 1966, pp. 198–228

27. W. F. Maunder, op. cit., p. 16

28. Wertheim, op. cit., pp. 173–4. Cf. Maunder's definition '(Underemployment is) . . . defined to exist when labour can be withdrawn from a certain line, leaving all co-operative factors unchanged without causing any decrease in final output', p. 11

29. The argument can be carried a step further if we accept that the characteristics of the economy in each of these sectors, following Maunder, are that the firm-type economy is dynamic and the bazaar economy is largely static. The types of unemployment which are brought about in the firm-type economy can be induced by the logical frictional and structural conditions in the economy. On the other hand, far more common in the bazaar sector are seasonal patterns of employment. Thus, for example, Castles explaining the labour employment pattern in the cigarette industry of Kudus, points out that workers in the industry tend to fluctuate occasionally in times of peak labour demand in agriculture by not coming to work at all. The close relationship of the agricultural and urban sectors has important ramifications, to be dealt with later, for the employment patterns of the city.

30. Geertz, 1962

31. Geertz, 1962, p. 32

32. Geertz, 1963, p. 30

33. Geertz, 1963, p. 31

34. Geertz, 1963, pp. 46–7

35. See S. H. Franklin, 'Systems of Production: Systems of Appropriation', *Pacific Viewpoint*, September, 1965, Vol. 6, No. 2, pp. 145–66

36. Cyril S. Belshaw, *Traditional Exchange and Modern Markets*, 1965, p. 80

37. Clifford Geertz, *Agricultural Involution. The Processes of Ecological Change in Indonesia*, 1963, p. 82

38. See Richard W. Redick, 'A Demographic and Ecological Study of Rangoon, Burma', 1961. Unpublished Ph.D. thesis, University of Chicago, for a discussion of this phenomena.

39. See C. Clark, 'The Economic Functions of a City in Relation to its Size', *Econometrica*, XIII, 1945

40. Eric E. Lampard, op. cit.

41. See Paul Goodman, *Like a conquered province: the moral ambiguity of America*, 1967

42. For instance, see Edward L. Ulman 'Regional Development and the Geography of Concentration', J. Friedmann and W. Alonso, op. cit., pp. 153–72, for striking evidence of this process of concentration in the United States

43. Keith Buchanan, 'Profiles of the Third World', *Pacific Viewpoint*, Vol. 5, No. 2, p. 107

44. Ibid., p. 108

45. Shanti Tangri, 'Urbanisation, Political Stability and Economic Growth' in Roy Turner (ed.), *India's Urban Future*, 1962, pp. 192–212

46. See Frantz Fanon, *The Damned*, 1963, pp. 121–63. We would add that Fanon's faith in the lumpen-proletariat is scarcely shared by Marx and Engels. See Marx' description of the manipulation of the lumpen-proletariat by the bourgeoisie in the 1848 Paris revolution: 'The Class Struggles in France 1848–1850' in Karl Marx and Frederick Engels, *Selected Works*, Vol. I, Moscow, 1951, p. 142

47. Ibid., op. 104

48. Richard M. Morse, 'Latin American Cities: Aspects of Function and Structure' in Friedman and Alonso, op. cit., p. 379

49. André Gundar Frank, op. cit., 1967, p. 110

50. See N. S. Ginsburg, 'The Great City in Southeast Asia', *American Journal of Sociology*, March, 1955, Vol. 60, No. 5, p. 457. Also see Brian J. L. Berry, *Geography of Market Centers and Retail Distribution*, 1967, especially Chapters 5 and 7

51. Morse, op. cit., p. 379; citing Simon Rottenberg, 'Note on the Economics of Urbanisation in Latin America', United Nations Document E/CN–12–URB/6-UNESCO/SS/URB/LA/6 (September 30, 1958), pp. 8–11

52. Is the labour-intensive traditional urban service sector, in fact, acting as a training ground, establishing commercial and urban attitudes, and reallocating the labour force more efficiently in Western terms? If it is, then it is acting as intermediary between the traditional and modern sectors. But, this presupposes that the bazaar sector in most Third World cities has significant elements of capitalist attitudes built into its structure. We have seen, however, that by its nature, it is an integral part of the traditional sector. The *pasar* system cannot then be relied upon to act as a technological, social or cultural bridge between the traditional and capitalist sectors. Although it operates cheek-by-jowl with the capitalist system in the cities, the *pasar* is in most cases as culturally insulated from the modern sector as the peasant sector in the countryside. Its values, like those of the peasant sector, as we have seen, are at least as solidly based on social and community factors as on commercial. There are, however, varying degrees of this insulation within the Third World—in fact, as we shall see, in some countries the labour-absorptive traditional urban sector scarcely exists as an independent entity.

53. Bruce H. Herrick, *Urban Migration and Economic Development in Chile*, 1965, p. 67

54. See A. O. Hirschman, *The Strategy of Economic Development*, 1958, for a discussion of this position

55. See G. C. Allen, *A Short Economic History of Modern Japan*, London, Unwin University Books, 1962, p. 125, Also see Tsunehiko Watanabe, 'Economic Aspects of Dualism in the Industrial Development of Japan', *Economic Development and Cultural Change*, April, 1965, Vol. XIII, No. 3, pp. 293–312. His statement that: 'In general, the combination of dualism with adoption of capital-using techniques in the industrial development of Japan, could be identified as one of the key explanations for her rapid growth' (p. 308), would appear broadly to support the Hirschman position.

56. Sir Arthur Lewis, op. cit., 1967, pp. 21–2

57. Nathan Keyfitz, 'Political-Economic Aspects of Urbanisation in South and Southeast Asia', in Philip M. Hauser and Leo F. Schnore, *The Study of Urbanisation*, 1965, p. 296

58. A reading of Chayanov, A. V. Chayanov, '*The theory of peasant economy*', edited by Daniel Thorner (et al.), Homewood, Illinois, American Economic Association, 1966, makes it clear that this problem stems from the inability to develop new concepts for the study of these 'peasant' systems. See also S. H. Franklin, 1965, op. cit.

59. Clifford Geertz, *Peddlers and Princes*, op. cit., pp. 48ff

60. Ibid., p. 48

61. Ibid., p. 49

62. Ibid., pp. 49–50 (footnote)

63. Ibid., p. 31

64. Ibid., p. 49 (footnote)

65. Ibid., p. 50

66. This does not mean that no outlets existed in the Cuban and other Latin American cities in the service sector. However, the proliferation of occupations within the sector was based not on traditional tertiary activity, but on Western-oriented goods, services and other needs— bellboys, taxi-drivers, touts, prostitutes, shoe-shine boys and so on—and did not create the great number of consequent labour-absorbing activities as in the traditional *pasar*. See also Oscar Lewis, *La Vida*, 1967, for a description of the way of life of people employed in these occupations.

67. It is not easy to quantify this argument. Even in the 1953 Cuban Census occupation figures are not broken down in sufficient detail for conclusive argument. The Census shows that 47 per cent of the active Cuban population were in agricultural jobs; 18 per cent artisans and machine operators; 8 per cent sellers of goods (some of whom were possibly in the traditional sectors); 5 per cent supervisors and executives; 4 per cent professional groups. The census also looked at employment in broader sectoral groups. According to this breakdown, 41 per cent were

in agriculture; 17 per cent in manufacturing; 12 per cent in commerce (shops, warehouses, banks, etc.); 20 per cent in other services and government; 10 per cent in construction, transport and communications, other public utilities and mining. Figures from the *Censos de Poblacion, Viviendas y Electoral*, Oficina Nacional de los Censos Demografica y Electoral, 28 February, 1953, La Habana, 1955, pp. XLI–XLII

Neither division seems to leave much room for traditional tertiary urban activity except perhaps in the category of 'sellers of goods'—a mere 6 per cent of all occupations. The evidence is not conclusive but the conjuncture of a number of the features of the Cuban economy —the extremely high proportion of commercialized farming centred around sugar; the low level of subsistence crop production and the high level of food imports; and finally the small number engaged in traditional tertiary activity—seem to support the arguments presented in this section.

68. For instance, K. B. Griffin, 'Reflections on Latin American Development', *Oxford Economic Papers*, 18, 1, March, 1966, and A. Gundar Frank, op. cit., pp. 248–54

PART TWO

THE TEST OF REALITY

☆ 4 ☆

An Aspect of Urbanization in Southeast Asia: The Process of Cityward Migration

In developing areas the sequence of events leading to urbanization is perhaps different from that noted in 19th century Europe and North America.[1]

INTRODUCTION

IN THE period since 1945 the urban areas of Southeast Asia[2] have grown rapidly. As Table 1 reveals, the increase of towns of over 100,000 population has been well in excess of the increase of the total population with the one exception of the Philippines. Such a rapid growth has not always been characteristic of these urban areas. It has been estimated that . . .

Between 1800 and 1850 the large city population of Asia increased by about 25 per cent in contrast with an increase of 184 per cent in Europe and America combined. Between 1850 and 1900, Asian large city population increased by about 60 per cent as contrasted with an increase of over 210 per cent in Europe and America. In the first half of this century, however, the large city population of Asia has grown by almost 450 per cent as compared with only 160 per cent in Europe and America.[3]

This urban growth has not been distributed evenly among the various size categories of the urban areas. In general, it is the larger cities which have accounted for a sizeable portion of the numerical increase in town populations—a trend given early emphasis by the nature of the colonial economy—continuing today as the most characteristic feature of Southeast Asian urbanization. The tendency for the urban hierarchy of many

G 97

Southeast Asian countries is to be dominated by '. . . one great metropolis, "the primate city", a great city which dominates the urban situation'.[4] Table 1 suggests that while the percentage increases of the larger towns is not always as fast as the

TABLE 1

SOUTHEAST ASIA

GROWTH OF URBAN POPULATION IN SELECTED COUNTRIES

Country	Period	Per cent Increase of Towns 100,000 +	Per cent Increase of Largest Town	Per cent Increase of Total Population
Burma (1)	1941–1958	40·5 (2·2)[a]	35·3 (1·4)	20·3 (1·1)
Federation of Malaya (2)	1947–1957	51·8 (5·1)	79·7 (7·9)	27·9 (2·7)
Indonesia (3)	1930–1960	170·6 (5·6)[b]	357·7 (11·9)	60·6 (2·0)
Philippines (4)	1948–1960	44·3 (3·4)[c]	16·5 (1·3)	43·4 (3·6)
Thailand (5)	1947–1960	118·0 (8·4)	115·0 (8·2)	59·2 (4·5)

Notes: [a] Figures in brackets are the yearly rates of increase.
  [b] This figure is calculated for the *Kotapradja* of Indonesia which include some towns of below 100,000 population.
  [c] The low rate of increase in the Philippines is probably not correct, and when it is possible to analyse the 1960 Census in detail it seems likely that the rate of increase will be much higher.

Sources: (1) United Nations Department of Economic and Social Affairs, *Demographic Yearbook*, 1960, New York, p. 306.
  (2) H. Fell, *1957 Population Census of Malaya*, Report Number 14, Kuala Lumpur, p. 8.
  (3) William A. Withington, 'The Kotapradja or "King Cities" of Indonesia', *Pacific Viewpoint*, Vol. 4, Number 1, March, 1963, p. 76.
  (4) The United Nations Department of Economic and Social Affairs, *Demographic Yearbook*, 1960, New York, pp. 323–4.
  (5) Thailand. Central Statistical Office, National Economic Development Board, *Thailand Population Census 1960. Whole Kingdom*, Bangkok, 1962, pp. 4–7.

rest of the town population, they are still accounting for a considerable portion of the increased urban population. In fact, the slower rates of growth of some of the larger cities such as Bangkok and Manila is almost certainly due to the out-movement of population from the crowded city core. Thus, Manila City grew by 109·3 per cent between 1947 and 1960: in the same period Quezon City on its boundaries grew by a marked increase of 268·5 per cent. The slowing down of the growth rate of the large cities in some cases simply indicates the growth of suburbanization.

There is scant evidence on what have been the main components in this considerable increase of population in urban areas. Natural increase has been of some importance although comprehensive data on rural–urban differentials in fertility and mortality are extremely difficult to find. For instance, evidence on fertility differentials is contradictory, and it is difficult to establish a clear pattern. Some evidence suggests that fertility may be lower in urban than in rural areas, but at the same time there are some indications that family size tends to rise with income[5] in many of the Southeast Asian countries. If this is so, it might count as a factor in increasing urban fertility as urban incomes are almost invariably higher than rural ones in Southeast Asia. However, the greatest factor in increasing the populations of the Southeast Asian cities has probably been the reduction in the mortality rate, particularly the infant mortality rate.[6]

Another factor contributing to the increase in city populations has been the expansion of the size of urban areas. In the period between 1947 and 1957 Kuala Lumpur expanded from 18 square miles to 30 square miles in size and in the process incorporated villages which had formerly been adjacent to the city.[7] Heeren has described a somewhat similar process in the case of Djakarta.[8] Another aspect of this growth of city populations has been the creation of new 'satellite towns' which are, in many cases, simply new residential suburbs of the city. Typical of such areas are Petaling Jaya, close to Kuala Lumpur; Kebajoran Baru, adjacent to Djakarta and Quezon City, which is now the capital of the Philippines. In addition to these middle-class areas, there is a proliferation of squatter areas surrounding the city which has sometimes induced city authorities to expand city boundaries in order to provide better living conditions.

While there is no doubt that natural increase and urban extension have accounted for some of this increase, it is impossible to disagree with U.N.E.S.C.O. when it comments that 'rural–urban migration has undoubtedly accounted for the overwhelming share of urban growth in the region'.[9] Yet,

99

surprisingly, it is the one component of population growth in urban areas which is most inadequately treated. Historically, of course, rural–urban migration has always contributed the major part of the urban growth of Southeast Asia. In the period after 1800 when the majority of cities in Southeast Asia were being established by the colonial powers, and even in cities not established by colonial powers, such as Bangkok, the majority of cities of Southeast Asia were being peopled by rural migrants. But, in many cases, they were not internal migrants but rather immigrants from other countries—Europeans, Chinese, Indians and Arabs. The most numerous group were the Chinese, and they tended to assume a dominant numerical and commercial position in the cities. Surprisingly most of them came from rural backgrounds[10] and yet they adapted to the urban areas with great ability. Thus the colonial city was an alien creation to the local groups whose migration to the city was not extensive during the colonial period.

However, the post-World War II period has seen the rise of the political independence of these powers and with it the assumption of control by the indigenous groups. The cities are no longer alien and thus there has been created a psychological and political situation which is encouraging to the rural migrant. In addition, the independent powers have endeavoured to create new industries in the city which have provided greater job opportunities for the rural migrants. Virtually every country in Southeast Asia is now experiencing a rapid rural–urban movement. A 1954 Djakarta survey showed 73 per cent of the Indonesian househeads interviewed were born outside the city;[11] in 1960, 26·6 per cent were born outside Bangkok;[12] 47·7 per cent outside Phnom Penh;[13] 34 per cent outside Singapore[14] and an estimated 50 per cent outside Kuala Lumpur.[15] These figures clearly indicate the importance of in-migration to the cities of Southeast Asia. The rest of this paper is concerned with the patterns of rural–urban migration, and in particular, with investigating the question of whether the rural–urban movements in Southeast Asia have any similarities with those that occurred in Western Europe during the industrial revolution. The next section investigates the character of rural–urban migration in Western Europe and puts forward some generalized conclusions with which to compare the process in Southeast Asia.

FORMULATING A EUROPEAN MODEL

The problems of constructing a model of the mechanisms and dynamics of rural–urban migration in Western Europe during the period of the industrial revolution are numerous. First, there is the problem of finding and assembling population data which covers the whole of Western Europe. Despite the lack of census material there are several studies on three Western European countries which are of great value; studies by Redford,[16] Smelser,[17] Ravenstein,[18] and Saville,[19] of population movements during the English industrial revolution; the results of research by Thomas,[20] Hagerstrand,[21] and Pred,[22] in Sweden, and the work of Pickney,[23] Wrigley,[24] and Dickinson,[25] in France, Germany and Belgium. A study of these sources provides a considerable body of evidence on the nature of rural–urban migration from which a broad model of rural–urban migration can be constructed.

Secondly, it is difficult to construct a model of rural–urban migration which incorporates the uneven temporal and regional impact of the industrial revolution. The economic, social and technical changes wrought by the industrial revolution began first in Great Britain during the eighteenth century, came later to Northern France and Belgium and did not really occur in Germany until after 1871. Its impact was felt even later in the northern countries such as Sweden, and not until the twentieth century in Eastern Europe and Russia. This 'uneven time impact' unquestionably influenced the type and manner of rural urban migration which occurred in various countries.

There is also the third problem of the time span of the industrial revolution. There is, for instance, clear evidence that the type and character of rural–urban migration changed considerably as the industrial revolution progressed. Thus, in some countries, seasonal migration to the cities changed to permanent migration; single migration to family migration; and male migration to female migration. Finally, there is the debatable question of the relationship between industrialism and the growth of towns. While there may be no reason to argue with Davis and Golden's claim that the 'achievement of high levels of urbanization anywhere in the world had to wait for *(the relatively short periods of)** the industrial revolution'[26] if it is applied on a world-wide level, it should be remembered that in Western Europe there already existed large cities such as Paris and London which grew rapidly at the same time as the newer industrial towns such as Manchester.

Broadly speaking, then, migration to the cities of Western Europe varied with each regional and temporal stage of the industrial revolution. The first stage of migration which had been occurring for many centuries was the movement of seasonal labour into the larger cities. Thus Redford reports that much of 'the general dock-labour around Paris . . . was done by seasonal migrants from Brittany and Normandy'.[27] There was also seaosnal movements of masons from the central massif areas to Paris. Such patterns of seasonal labour were common in other cities. In England in the second half of the eighteenth century when country factories were being established they tended to employ a highly mobile transitory labour force who habitually sought seasonal occupations. Redford comments that the early mill-owners had great difficulty in getting such people to settle down, and in fact recruiters were sent into the country to obtain labour.[28]

In these early phases such labour tended to be single and dominantly male. Thus the beginnings of rural to urban movement in the early phases of the industrial revolution were essentially based on impermanent populations who took some time to stabilize in the urban areas.

The second type of movement—the shift to permanent residence in the city—occurred during what may be called the 'main' period of the industrial revolution; the period of industrial concentration based on steam power, coal and iron production which occurred during the nineteenth century. This period can be said to have induced rural–urban migration from two sources. First there was a movement of industrial workers from declining industrial areas to newer ones. Secondly, agricultural workers were also moving to the cities in search of jobs. In most of Britain 'The motive force controlling the migra-

* The words in italics are mine.

tion was the positive attraction of the industry rather than the negative repulsion of agriculture'[29] despite the fact that the years between 1815 and 1850 were depression years in agriculture. Most of the migration to English cities during this period was family migration. In the case of the industrial migrant 'the father of a family would in most cases pursue a declining trade as long as he could, hoping for a turn in the tide; in the last resort he moved with his family to the nearest town. The unspecialized labour of the children was there readily absorbed.'[30]

Because of the family nature of this migration it was probably much less selective in terms of sex and age groups than was the later migration. Migration was in most cases short-distance migration characterized by a step pattern. '. . . The great majority of migrants went only a short distance, and migration into any centre of attraction having a wide sphere of influence was not a simple transference of people from the circumference of a circle to its centre, but an exceedingly complex wave-like motion.'[31] In general the largest cities attracted the largest proportion of the urban population growth at this time. Thus the London County area grew by one and half million population between 1800 and 1850 while Manchester, the centre of the industrialism of the north, only increased its population by 279,000.[32] In addition the volume and length of population movement to the cities was a positive function of city size.[33] Finally, there is the important role that specific cultural groups such as the Irish played in the patterns of rural–urban migration. Thus the seasonal visits of the Irish harvesters to England was the beginning which eventually led to permanent settlement in England. This pattern, coupled with the severe economic conditions in Ireland, led to a mass movement of Irish labourers to England, the majority of whom settled in the large towns.[34]

Finally, there is the third period of the industrial revolution when population movements to the cities were increasingly characterized by a dominance of females. In England and Wales, Saville points out that, 'In the second half of the nineteenth century . . . women were more migratory than men. Generally by the end of the century, the urban areas showed a higher proportion of females to males, at all ages, than the rural areas.'[35] This was largely because in the rural areas employment opportunities for females were declining faster than those for males and thus women were being pushed out of the countryside at a faster rate. Thomas supports this pattern with evidence for Sweden for a somewhat later period.

This then is a brief résumé of the main characteristics of rural–urban migration during the period of the industrial revolution in Western Europe. Six main features of rural–urban migration emerge.

(*a*) The largest cities tended to attract the greatest number of migrants though not necessarily growing as fast as the newer industrial cities.

(*b*) Rural–urban migration was generally short-distance migration with the one proviso that the larger the city, the greater distance from which it would attract migrants.

(*c*) In terms of migration differentials three main features can be observed;

    (i) During the earlier part of the revolution the migration pattern tended to be made up of single seasonal workers. This changed to a pattern of family migration during the 'main' phase of the industrial revolution, although during the later parts of the industrial revolution, single migration was more characteristic.

    (ii) Migrants tended to be concentrated into what have been called the 'migration prone' age groups between 15–35 years although this pattern was not so clear during the family phase of rural–urban movement.

    (iii) The sex differentials of the migrants varied considerably from country to country and phase to phase of the industrial revolution. During the earliest phases it was largely male dominated, but later it was evenly balanced between males and females and finally passing into a phase where migration was dominated by females.

(*d*) There was a tendency for certain cultural groups such

as the Irish to figure prominently in the rural–urban movements.

(*e*) Finally if the simple, 'push-pull' framework of motivation for migration is accepted, it seems clear that the 'pull' factors of increasing opportunities for employment in the new industrial cities and large towns acted as a far more important motivating force than any 'push' factors such as the decline of agricultural employment opportunities.

In the next section of the paper a comparison is made between the process and dynamics of rural–urban migration in Europe described above and cityward movement in Southeast Asia today.

SOUTHEAST ASIAN COMPARISONS

As has already been mentioned, data on the various aspects of rural–urban movement in Southeast Asia is scarce, but enough information can be culled from recent census material and some specific surveys of rural–urban migration to enable some comparisons with the European model. It would be reasonable to assume that the different cultural milieu, the different historical era and the technical improvements of the present day would have meant that the pattern of rural–urban migration in Southeast Asia would vary strikingly from that of the industrial revolution in Europe, but as the following analysis suggests there are striking similarities.

(1) Rural–urban Migration and the Larger Cities

Most evidence suggests that the larger cities of Southeast Asia today are attracting a greater proportion of the rural migrants than the smaller cities. It is true that evidence on the growth rates of the larger cities suggests that they are not growing as fast as the smaller cities in many cases. But this growth pattern must be seen in the context of increasing suburbanization and the establishment of satellite towns on the fringes of many of these larger cities. For instance, while the population of Manila City grew by only 166,000 between 1948 and 1960, the population of Metropolitan Manila increased by almost 1 million people.[36] Care should be taken in viewing such a process as similar to the pattern of conurbation which occurred in urbanized areas such as Manchester and London during the industrial revolution, for the process of urban expansion is advancing into agricultural land and incorporating agricultural villages, not the merging of urban areas. Thus although the growth rates of some of the larger cities may be slowing down, in the total metropolitan areas there can be little doubt that the rate of increase exceeds other urban areas.

(2) Migration and Distance

One of the most generally accepted features of migration during the industrial revolution was that it tended to be short-distance migration with the one provision that the larger the city, the greater the area from which it drew its migrants. In general present-day patterns in Southeast Asia seem remarkably similar. For instance, in 1960 approximately 50 per cent of the population which had been born outside Phranakhorn Chang-wad (which incorporates the population of Bangkok and Thonburi Municipalities) came from within a 50-mile radius of the city.[37] In Singapore an analysis of the exchange of identity cards showed that the majority of migrants had come from the adjacent state of Johore.[38] In a survey of Malay migration to Kuala Lumpur carried out by the author in 1962-3, 20 per cent of the migrants had come from the state in which Kuala Lumpur is located and the majority of these migrants came from kampongs within 30 miles of the city.[39] The 1953 survey of migrants to Djakarta reported that 21 per cent of the Javanese migrants to the city came from the *Kabupaten* of Bogor, a regency which is only about half an hour from the city by bus or train.[40] The highest percentage of migrants who had been born in a surrounding district were the 40 per cent of Cambodian national migrants in Phnom Penh city who came from the Kandal province.[41]

Historically, of course, the short-distance migration law did not apply to the Southeast Asian cities at least from the colonial era onwards. During the initial phases of the establishment of colonial cities in Southeast Asia, the cities were peopled by migrants who frequently travelled great distances; the Chinese were by far the most ubiquitous and sometimes travelled the greatest distances; but there were Indians, Arabs and Europeans as well. In addition, at least in some areas such as Java, there was a movement of local people to the cities, but in general the cities remained alien creations attracting alien migrants. With the passing of immigration restrictions, the cities of Southeast Asia can no longer grow from such long-range migration and the patterns of migration are swinging to the characteristic short-distance migration of the West European industrial revolution. Even today the cities still attract migrants from considerable distances such as the *samlor* drivers who move from Northeast Thailand to Bangkok and the Minangkabaus movement from Sumatra to Djakarta. Such movement, it is suggested, may be as much due to earlier established patterns of cityward movement and of the cultural distinctiveness of such groups as to the superior attraction of the city.

(3) Step Migration

A third feature of the migration patterns during the industrial revolution was a tendency for people to move to the larger cities in a series of moves from rural to small town and then to larger urban area in a pattern which has been labelled 'step migration'. Once again historically Southeast Asia has not followed this pattern entirely. Many of the Chinese who came from long distances originally made the transition from rural to urban environment in one step. Today it is difficult to establish whether 'step migration' is more prevalent. In the Malay migrant survey carried out in Kuala Lumpur over 90 per cent of migrants had moved more than twice before settling in the city. This probably, however, reflects the role that Kuala Lumpur plays as the political capital of the Federation. The post-Independence period has seen the gradual disappearance of the 'expatriate' administrators and the adoption of a government policy which is replacing them largely by Malays. Thus there has been a shift of many public servants, who have seen many moves to Kuala Lumpur.[42] However, the 1964 Djakarta survey reports 'that by far the great part (80·4 per cent) of the migrants moved directly to the capital'.[43] In view of the high percentage of direct migrants reported in the Djakarta survey in contradistinction to the Kuala

Lumpur experience, the evidence might suggest that improved transport facilities, particularly road transport, have greatly eased the problems of the migrant trip, and that improved education has increased the knowledge of the urban environment, making it easier for the migrant to settle in the larger city. But it would seem that until further evidence is available, a conclusion on the patterns of Southeast Asian step migration will have to be left in abeyance.

(4) Migration Demographic Differentials

One of the clearest indications of rural–urban migration patterns has been the rural–urban differences in sex ratios. It has been noted that rural–urban migration during the industrial revolution went through a series of phases from dominantly male migration, to an evenly balanced migration and finally to a largely female migration. As Table 2 shows the majority of Southeast Asian large cities have sex ratios which are much more heavily weighted in favour of males than the national figures. Only part of this male dominance in the cities can be explained by the fact that, with the exception of Cambodia and Indonesia, the national sex ratios have a higher ratio of males to females than is characteristic in most Western countries. More significant, perhaps, is the influence of immigrant communities, particularly the Chinese, for these communities generally have highly unbalanced sex ratios heavily weighted in favour of males in addition to having a high percentage of their population concentrated in the main urban areas (see Table 3). Even allowing for these above factors the male (with the exception of the Philippines) dominant sex ratios of the urban areas points to a dominantly male migration from rural to urban areas. This is further emphasized by the tendency of the populations to become more masculine as the localities become more urban which—the U.N.E.S.C.O. Report confirms—'. . . reflects primarily the sex composition of migrants from rural areas and villages to towns and cities'. [44]

A further indication of not only the male dominant character of this migration, but also its age selectivity can be obtained from the age specific sex ratios shown in Table 4 and the age divergency graphs (Figure 9). In 1957 the U.N.E.S.C.O.

TABLE 2
SEX RATIOS OF LARGEST CITY AND
CAPITAL OR GROUP OF CITIES OF 100,000 +

Country	Year of Census	Males per 100 Females
BURMA (1)	1953	104
Cities of 100,000 +		111
INDONESIA (2)	1961	97
Djakarta		105
SINGAPORE (1)	1947	122
Singapore City		122
THAILAND (3)	1960	104
Cities of 100,000 +		104
FEDERATION OF MALAYA (4)	1957	106
Kuala Lumpur		113
SARAWAK (1)	1947	101
Kuching		106
NORTH BORNEO (1)	1951	107
Sandakan		119
BRUNEI (1)	1951	122
Belait (12,551)		155
PHILIPPINES (5)	1960	101
Manila City		93
CAMBODIA (6)	1959	100
Phnom Penh		105

Sources: (1) The data for sex ratios of Burma, Singapore, Sarawak, North Borneo and Brunei was taken from Philip M. Hauser (ed.), *Urbanization in Asia and the Far East*, U.N.E.S.C.O., Paris, 1957, pp. 124–5.

(2) Department of Foreign Affairs, Republic of Indonesia, *Indonesia, 1962*, p. 38.

(3) Central Statistical Office, Economic Development Board Thailand, *Thailand Population Census, 1960*, Bangkok, pp. 4–7.

(4) H. Fell, *1957 Population Census of the Federation of Malaya*, Report Number 14, Kuala Lumpur, 1960, pp. 53–5.

(5) Bureau of the Census and Statistics, *Census of the Philippines, 1960*, 'Manila', Vol. 1, Manila, 1960, pp. 30–2.

(6) The total population figures for Cambodia were taken from Tan-kim Huon, *Géographie du Cambodge*, Phnom Penh, 1961, p. 72. The figures for Phnom Penh came from an unpublished cyclostyled document incorporating the 1959 Cambodian Census results for Phnom Penh.

TABLE 3

Numbers of Chinese in Selected Southeast Asian Countries and some Features of their Urban Patterns

Country	Date of Population Estimate	Size of Chinese Population	Chinese as a Percentage of Total Population	Percentage of each Country's Chinese Population Living in Major Urban Area	Chinese as a Percentage of Total Population Living in Major Urban Area	Sex Ratios of Chinese in Urban Area
Indonesia	1950s	2,500,000	2·5	12·0	10·2	—
Thailand	1960	384,000	1·5	51·3	9·2	155·9
Philippines	1948	250,000	1·0	36·0	3·4	136·3
Burma	1950s	300,000	1·5	—	—	—
Federation of Malaya	1957	2,333,756	37·0	8·3	63·4	103·0
Cambodia	1959	275,000	5·6	22·8	17·6	116·2

Notes: Accurate contemporary figures of the Chinese in Southeast Asian countries are difficult to locate. Few national censuses identify the Chinese population by any other form than place of birth which means the Chinese populations are frequently underestimated in such documents.

Sources: National censuses cited in the other tables were used in the preparation of this Table.

TABLE 4

RATIO OF MALES TO FEMALES FOR TOTAL POPULATION
AND MAIN CITY BY SPECIFIC AGE GROUPS

PHILIPPINES (1969) (1)	Total Population	Manila City
15–24	102·4	73·6
25–34	95·4	92·7
35–44	97·4	96·4
Total Population	101·4	93·2
CAMBODIA (1959) (2)	Total Population	Phnom Penh
15–24	96·3	98·2
25–34	94·3	104·3
35–44	97·5	120·7
Total Population	99·7	105·0
THAILAND (1960) (3)	Total Population	Phranakhorn (Bangkok)
15–24	101·4	108·6
25–34	99·5	106·1
35–44	101·3	108·0
Total Population	100·3	103·7
FEDERATION OF MALAYA (1957) (4)	Total Population	Kuala Lumpur
15–24	99·3	117·6
25–34	99·0	116·0
35–44	110·5	123·0
Total Population	106·0	113·0

Sources: (1) The Manila figures were calculated from Bureau of Census and Statistics, *Census of the Philippines, 1960*, 'Manila', Vol. 1, Manila, 1960, pp. 30–3.
The total population figures were calculated from United Nations Department of Economic and Social Affairs, *Demographic Yearbook, 1960*, New York, 1960, pp. 216–17.

(2) The total population figures were calculated from Tan-kim Huon, *Géographie du Cambodge*, Phnom Penh, 1961, p. 72. The figures for Phnom Penh were calculated from an unpublished cyclostyled document incorporating the 1959 Cambodian Census results for Phnom Penh.

(3) The figures for Thailand were taken from the Central Statistical Office, Economic Development Board, Thailand, *Thailand Population Census, 1960*, Bangkok, 1960. The figures for Phranakhorn Changwad which is made up largely of Bangkok Municipality from *Thailand Population Census, 1960, Changwad Series, Changwad Phranakhorn*.

(4) The figures for the Federation of Malaya and Kuala Lumpur were taken from H. Fell, *1957 Population Census of the Federation of Malaya*, Report Number 14 and *1957 Population Census, State of Selangor*, Report Number 2, Kuala Lumpur, 1960.

Report commented: 'The excess of males over females in urban areas is greatest, in most cases, at ages 15–59, and more particularly at ages 15–39,'[45] and in general this is supported by both Table 4 and the divergency graphs. What is interesting is the exception of the Philippines which has a clear majority of females in the city and a striking dominance of females in the age group 15–24. Other countries also show indications of a breakdown of the male dominant sex ratios in this younger age group. Whether or not this increase in the number of females in urban areas represents the beginning of a trend towards the female dominant pattern of migration already accomplished in the Philippines is an interesting question. Certain evidence from Cambodia suggests that some of this female movement may be marriage movement. For instance, there were over twice as many married women in the age group between 15 and 24 years as men. Thus a pattern is established of a young single man moving first to the city and after he has earned enough money and established himself he sends back to his village for a wife to be found for him. His new wife then joins him in the city. Evidence for this pattern has been provided by the Kuala Lumpur survey.

However, there is no doubt that the male dominated rural–urban migration patterns which had characterized the Philippines in 1948 have changed dramatically to a dominantly female movement to the city (Figure 9c). The reasons for this movement of females have been suggested by Hunt.[46] First, the rapid increase of manufacturing, much of it located in Manila City, has created favourable employment opportunities for the females who are frequently found more efficient for the routine work involved in industrial assembly. Secondly, we must consider the large numbers of females who pass on to college education in the Philippines and the fact that these institutions are highly concentrated in Manila City. Finally, the female movement represents far-seated social changes in the nature of Filipino society in which the equality of the sexes is becoming an increasingly important feature. Thus the dominantly male character of rural–urban migration in Southeast Asia is similar to the earlier phases of the industrial revolution and there are even indications that if the Filipino pattern becomes

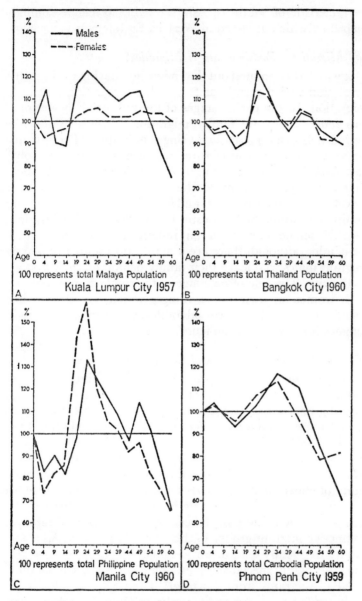

Figure 9. Divergency-graph of age structure, selected Southeast Asian cities

characteristic of Southeast Asia the swing to female-dominant migration which occurred in Western Europe may occur also.

(5) Migration—Family or Single Migration?

It was earlier pointed out that migration during the industrial revolution varied greatly as to whether it was single or family migration. In the earlier stages of the industrial revolution, it was more frequently family migration, though in the later period it became increasingly single migration. There is little evidence on this aspect of rural–urban migration from Southeast Asia. The Kuala Lumpur and Djakarta surveys indicate that about 50 per cent of the migrants were married and travelled with their families, and it has been suggested that such family migration 'may constitute the "normal" migrational type'.[47] Single men form an important component of the remainder, although there are a significant number of married migrant males who leave their family behind on their first visit to the city. The role of marriage of the single men in the town with women in their home villages which has already been mentioned may be of considerable significance in bringing females into the urban milieu.[48]

(6) Rural–urban Migration and Cultural Distinctiveness

One of the features of the movement to cities during the industrial revolution was that not all of the movement fitted into the neat set of laws elaborated by Ravenstein.[49] In particular there was the movement of distinct cultural groups such as the Irish, which was partly motivated by the grinding poverty in their homeland, partly motivated by earlier patterns of seasonal agricultural migration to England and the possibility of cheap boat transport. Such movement, of course, did not conform in all its characteristics to many of the so-called migration laws. There have been many examples of culturally distinctive migrant groups in the cities of Southeast Asia. Such groups frequently tend to travel the longest distances and have the most highly specialized jobs. Some examples are the movement of migrants from Northeast Thailand to Bangkok and their tendency to group in *samlor* driving;[50] the large community of Boyans, from the small island of Bawean off the coast of Java, heavily concentrated in the driving and occupations which are concerned with horse racing;[51] and the movement of Minangkabaus from Sumatra to Djakarta where they tend to have a large proportion of the better government and clerical jobs.[52] It is not possible to explain the migration of such groups, frequently over long distances, purely in economic terms. Frequently they have a type of culture which can be said to be 'migrant prone'. Thus the Minangkabau group are characterized by a matriarchial social structure in which land passes through the female line. Such a situation does not offer the male many economic opportunities, and he frequently moves to the city. Such out-migration causes no major dislocation in the social and economic structure of the community from which he departs; in fact such out-movement was recognized in the past as a formal institution of the society, which allowed men to travel away from the village—*merantau*.[53] There are many other examples in Southeast Asia of 'migrant prone' groups, and it would seem that any set of general characteristics of rural–urban migration would have to incorporate them in some way or other.

(7) *Migration Motivations*

Perhaps the most well-established generalization on the nature of Southeast Asian rural–urban migrations, next to the statement that such migration is largely male-dominated, has been the claim that such migration is generally motivated primarily by 'push' rather than 'pull' factors. This statement is reiterated again and again in many of the works on Asian migration. For instance, the U.N.E.S.C.O. publication reports —'It gives a clue to one of the most important features of Asian rural–urban migration, namely the *push* of people from the countryside to the cities rather than the pull of industrial and employment opportunities in urban areas.'[54] This is, of course, in direct contrast to the experience of the industrial revolution in Western Europe where there was close connection between the economic demands for labour exerted by the rapidly-growing urban industry and the growth of cities. It has also led to the statement that many of the countries of Southeast Asia are 'over-urbanized' because they have too high a level of urbanization in relation to the level of economic development.[55] Such a situation creates many of the problems of unemployment, social and economic discontent which characterize many of the Southeast Asian cities. Rural migrants come to the cities because of the pressure of population and lack of jobs in the rural areas only to find that a similar situation is in existence in the city. Thus rural poverty is replaced by urban poverty. The process has been chronicled not only academically but also in many of the writings of Southeast Asian novelists; in harrowing terms by Mochtar Lubis in Indonesia,[56] Kerima Polotan in the Philippines,[57] and in a more lighthearted manner in Anthony Burgess' trilogy of Malaya.[58]

Yet, despite all the problems that result from rural-to-urban migration, the process still goes on and at an apparently faster rate, and the cities grow bigger and bigger. The fact that the migration still continues does lead to a situation where the simple 'push–pull' hypothesis of rural–urban migration does not seem to be an entirely adequate framework within which to assess the whole process of migration.[59] As the Report of the Population Conference held in Teheran comments, the rapid increase in urban population should not be regarded merely as a demographic phenomenon 'but rather as part of the whole fabric of strains and tensions which is inherent in a rapid process of social change, unaccompanied by a corresponding pace of economic growth.'[60]

It is thus a condition of society which is responsible for increased mobility—increased education facilities and improved communications make the rural dweller far more aware of the urban environment. The growth of nationalism acutely fostered by the new governments make the rural dweller more aware of the role he has to play in the new state. Political instability associated with the process of imposing national unity frequently forces the rural dweller into the city. The associated problem of getting economic development off the ground at times of such political instability means that development is not rapid enough to suggest to the rural dweller that his opportunities will be better in the rural areas than in the city. Thus push-and-pull symptoms are simply evidences of a wider condition of society, but it does indicate that the model of

Western European rural–urban migration needs to be modified substantially in the Asian situation.

IMPLICATIONS FOR POLICY PLANNING FOR THE FUTURE OF SOUTHEAST ASIAN CITIES

The broad conclusions of this preliminary comparison of the patterns of rural–urban migration in Western Europe and Southeast Asia are obvious. In many of the specific details of rural–urban migration patterns the Southeast Asian migrations bear remarkable similarities. Migration has been shown to be largely short-distance migration in both areas; the larger cities are attracting more migrants; there are evidences of step migration; the question of whether migration is single or family migration still seems to be rather confused as is the evidence for Europe. There is a tendency for migrants to be generally in migratory age groups; similar patterns of certain cultural groups being more 'prone' to migration and there is even a trend (clearly evident in the Philippines) which seems to indicate an increasing tendency of migration to the cities to become female dominant.

It is only in the general context of the motivations for migration that Southeast Asia seems to be different, but even here there is at least the factor of a general condition of society which is conducive to rural–urban migration. This is not to say that Southeast Asian governments view the process of rural–urban migration with favour. Many take the view that such a process is unhealthy, not only because of the social and economic erosion it causes in rural communities, but also because of the problem of urban overcrowding, poverty and unemployment which occurs in the cities. This is sometimes associated with an almost idealistic belief that the rural life is somehow morally better and the increasing urbanization will lead to a steady corruption of society. There are modern day Cobbetts as well. Such an attitude, although it can perhaps be best understood in the light of contemporary nationalisms and their attempt to build a truly indigenous culture in reaction against the alien impositions of colonialism, is scarcely realistic, in view of the inevitability of urbanization in the region. While it may be accepted that piecemeal policies of rural and urban development may stem the process in part, the most obvious need is for the collection of information in great detail, on the process of rural–urban migration. Only from such information can overall planning schemes be formulated which take advantage of the modern technological advances of this era, as well as increased government control. With such information and carefully designed plans which aim at increased industrialization in the cities as well as rural development, it may be possible to alleviate many of the pressing problems of rural–urban migration which characterize Southeast Asia today.

NOTES

1. Economic Commission for Asia and the Far East, *Draft Report of the Asian Population Conference*, Twentieth Session, March 2–17, 1964, Teheran, Iran (unpublished), p. 105

2. Southeast Asia is defined for the purpose of this paper as including Brunei, Burma, Cambodia, Indonesia, Laos, Malaysia, North Vietnam, the Philippines, South Vietnam and Thailand.

3. Philip M. Hauser (ed.), *Urbanization in Asia and the Far East*, U.N.E.S.C.O. Research Centre on the Social Implications of Industrialization in Southern Asia, Calcutta, 1957, p. 59

4. Ibid., p. 87. Other articles dealing with this aspect of Southeast Asia urbanization are D. W. Fryer, 'The Million City in Southeast Asia', *Geographical Review*, October, 1953, pp. 474–94; and Norton S. Ginsburg, 'The Great City in Southeast Asia', *American Journal of Sociology*, 60, 5, pp. 455–62

5. See, for instance, Department of Statistics, Federation of Malaya, *Household Budget Survey of the Federation of Malaya, 1957–58*, Kuala Lumpur, 1958

6. This is well illustrated by the Malaysian community in Singapore whose crude death rate fell from 17·8 per 1,000 in 1947 to 10 per 1,000 in 1957. See T. G. McGee, 'The Population of Malaysia: A Preliminary Analysis' in Wang Gungwu (ed.), *Malaysia: A Handbook*, London, 1964

7. See pp. 121–47

8. H. J. Heeren, 'The Urbanization of Djakarta', *Ekonomi dan Keuangan*, 11, November, 1955, p. 699

9. Philip M. Hauser (ed.), op. cit., p. 154

10. See Victor Purcell, *The Chinese in Southeast Asia*, London, 1961; G. William Skinner, *Chinese Society in Thailand: An Analytical History*, New York, 1957; and William H. Newell, *Treacherous River: A Study of Rural Chinese in North Malaya*, Kuala Lumpur, 1962

11. H. J. Heeren, op. cit., p. 702

12. Central Statistical Office, Economic Development Board, Thailand, *Thailand Population Census, 1960, Changwad Series, Changwad Phranakhorn*, Bangkok, 1961, pp. 8–11

13. Unpublished cylostyled document incorporating the 1959 Cambodian Census results for Phnom Penh

14. Department of Statistics, Singapore, *1957 Census of Population, Singapore*, Preliminary Release, No. 7, Singapore, 1959, pp. 2–3

15. See p. 126

16. Arthur Redford, *Labour Migration in England, 1800–1850*, London, 1926

17. Neil J. Smelser, *Social Change in the Industrial Revolution: An Application of Theory to the Lancashire Cotton Industry, 1770–1840*, London, 1959

18. E. G. Ravenstein, 'The Laws of Migration', *Journal of the Royal Statistical Society*, Vol. 48, June, 1885, pp. 167–235; 52, June, 1889, pp. 241–305

19. John Saville, *Rural Depopulation in England and Wales, 1851–1951*, London, 1957

20. Dorothy Swaine Thomas, *Social and Economic Aspects of Swedish Population Movements, 1750–1933*, New York, 1941

21. Torsten Hagerstrand, 'Migration and Area Survey of a Sample of Swedish Migration Fields and Hypothetical Considerations on Their Genesis' in David Hannerberg, Torsten Hagerstrand, Bruno Odeving, *Migration in Sweden: A Symposium*, Lund Studies in Geography, Series B, Human Geography, 13, Lund, 1957

22. Allan Pred, *The External Relations of Cities during the 'Industrial Revolution'*, The University of Chicago, Department of Geography, Research Paper, Number 76, Chicago, 1962

23. David H. Pickney, 'Migrations to Paris during the Second Empire', *The Journal of Modern History*, XXV, 1, March, 1953, pp. 1–12

24. E. A. Wrigley, *Industrial Growth and Population*, Cambridge, 1961

25. Robert E. Dickinson, *The West European City*, London, 1951

26. Kingsley Davis and Hilda Hertz Golden, 'Urbanization and the Development of Pre-Industrial Areas', *Economic Development and Cultural Change*, Vol. 3, 1954–5, p. 8

27. Arthur Redford, 1926, op. cit., p. 4

28. Ibid., pp. 20–1

29. Ibid., p. 21

30. Ibid., p. 160

31. Ibid., p. 160

32. G. D. H. Cole and Raymond Postgate, *The Common People, 1746–1946*, London, 1963, p. 137

33. Robert E. Dickinson, *The West European City*, London, 1951, pp. 447–8

34. Arthur Redford, op. cit., Chapters VIII and IX

35. John Saville, op. cit., p. 31

36. Carlos P. Ramos, 'Manila's Metropolitan Problem', *Philippine Journal of Public Administration*, April, 1961, Vol. 5, Number 2, p. 92

37. Central Statistical Office, Economic Development Board, Thailand,

Thailand Population Census, 1960, Changwad Series, Changwad Phranakhorn, Bangkok, 1961, pp. 8–11

38. See T. G. McGee, 'Malays in the City: A New Social Structure for Malaya?' Unpublished paper read to the Malaysia Society, Wellington, New Zealand, July 1, 1964, p. 2

39. Ibid., p. 6

40. H. J. Heeren, op. cit., p. 703

41. Unpublished cyclostyled document incorporating the 1959 Cambodian Census results for Phnom Penh.

42. T. G. McGee, 1964, op. cit., p. 8

43. H. J. Heeren, op. cit., p. 704

44. Philip M. Hauser (ed.), op. cit., p. 108

45. Ibid., p. 109

46. Chester L. Hunt, 'Changing Sex Ratio in Philippine Cities'. Paper presented to the I.G.U. Regional Conference on Southeast Asia held at Kuala Lumpur, April, 1962

47. H. J. Heeren, op. cit., p. 705

48. T. G. McGee, 1964, op. cit., p. 7

49. E. G. Ravenstein, op. cit.

50. Robert B. Textor, 'From Peasant to Pedicab Driver', *Yale University Cultural Report Series*, 9, New Haven, 1961

51. Jacob Vredenbregt, 'Bawean Migrations: Some Preliminary Notes', *Bijdragen, Tot de Taal-, Land-, en Volkenkunde*, 120, 1964, pp. 109–37

52. Ruth T. McVey (ed.), *Indonesia*, New Haven, 1963

53. T. G. McGee, 1964, op. cit., pp. 6–7

54. Philip M. Hauser, op. cit., p. 133

55. See B. F. Hoselitz, 'Generative and Parasitic Cities', *Economic Development and Cultural Change*, III, 3, 1955

56. Mochtar Lubis, *Twilight in Djakarta* (trs. Claire Holt), London, 1963

57. Kerima Polotan, *The Hand of the Enemy*, Manila, 1962

58. Anthony Burgess, *Beds in the East*, London, 1959

59. See William Petersen, 'A General Typology of Migration', *American Sociological Review*, 23, 3, June, 1958, pp. 256–66

60. Economic Commission for Asia and the Far East, *Draft Report of the Asian Population Conference*, p. 91

☆ 5 ☆

The Cultural Role of Cities:
A Case Study of Kuala Lumpur

Modern colonial cities raise the interesting question whether they can reverse from the 'heterogenetic' to the 'orthogenetic' role. For the last one hundred or more years they have developed as outposts of imperial civilizations, but as the countries in which they are located achieve political independence, will the cities change their cultural roles and contribute more to the formation of a civilization indigenous to their areas?[1]

INTRODUCTION

REDFIELD AND SINGER have suggested that cities may be classified into two main types, according to the role they play in cultural change. First, there are the cities of orthogenetic transformation, cities in which culture is carried forward. Typical of such cities were the urban centres of the earlier civilizations in which the 'developmental cultural function was generally combined with the political power and administrative control'. The second group of cities are those of heterogenetic transformation, 'where local cultures are disintegrated and new integrations of mind and society are developed'. In cities of this kind, men are concerned with the market, with rational organization of production of goods, with expediential relations between the buyer and seller, ruler and ruled, and native and foreigner.'[2] This twofold division of cities has considerable relevance to Malaya, and in particular to the role that Kuala Lumpur, the nation's federal capital and largest city, will play as a focus and centre for the dissemination of a new Malayan culture.[3]

This paper attempts to investigate the validity of such a conception of the cultural role of cities when it is applied to Kuala Lumpur. Since it has not been possible to carry out any detailed sociological surveys, the techniques of investigation are necessarily limited. However, the analysis of statistical data contained in the Population Censuses of 1947 and 1957, Reports on the Elections, Municipal Reports and the Household Budget Survey of 1957, provide sufficient information with which to assess the political, social and economic character of the city. The available statistics have their limitations, and many of the comments on the orthogenetic or heterogenetic character of Kuala Lumpur, which are based on these statistics, must of necessity be value judgments. This in no way invalidates the general conclusions of the paper, for as Gunnar Myrdal has commented, there is every reason why value judgments 'should be used not only as premises for our policy conclusions, but also to determine the direction of positive research'.[4]

Prior to 1957, Kuala Lumpur, to the superficial observer, appeared to be a typical colonial city of the heterogenetic type. It was first and foremost a city of the technical order, growing from 'a raw and robustious Chinese mining centre' in the eighteen-sixties,[5] to become a colonial administrative centre of the Federated Malay States by 1896. With the rapid growth of European-owned tin mines and rubber estates in the early nineteen-hundreds, European commercial interests were also grafted on to the political and Chinese economic activities of the city. By 1948 it had become the capital of the newly formed Federation of Malaya. During the present century it has always been an immigrant-dominated city, looking as much outwards to the homelands of Europe and China as it did to the internal functioning of Malaya. With the independence of Malaya in 1957, a new role was thrust upon the city—an integrative role, not only as a political centre, but also as a disseminating point for a new Malayan culture, which attempts to integrate the various and diverse ethnic elements and cultures of the plural society of Malaya into something which is uniquely Malayan. The formulators of this policy of 'nation building'[6] were the new political and administrative elite; drawn from the ethnically mixed middle and upper classes, which grew so rapidly in Kuala Lumpur between 1947 and 1957.[7]

The factors which forced them to follow a policy which involved the breaking down of communal cultures, rather than a policy of 'cultural pluralism',[8] were induced by the ideas of the class to which they belonged. They are a new, racially mixed, secularized group which has, to a large extent, become integrated by its acceptance of Western values, and has broken away from the more tradition-directed values of the majority of the population of Malaya. A policy of integration arising from social upgrading seemed to be the only policy to follow. In addition, the balance of race groups within Malaya meant that any policy which imposed one culture at the expense of another would almost certainly meet with disaster. Finally, any policy which favoured one group more than another would seem too much like the old colonial policy of 'divide and rule', and this must be avoided at all costs.

Viewed within the context of the Malayan society and the desire to build up an image of a united Malayan nation state, this change of Kuala Lumpur from a heterogenetic to an orthogenetic city may seem relatively simple, but in reality it is not. This is partly because there is considerable doubt as to how far Kuala Lumpar really fits into the category of a heterogenetic city, or how much the population of Kuala Lumpur moved towards accepting an orthogenetic tradition between 1947 and 1957, and partly because there is no clear picture of the orthogenetic role which was to be imposed upon Kuala Lumpur. As such, the newly independent city's role in bringing about cultural integration cannot be said to be transitional from heterogenetic to orthogenetic, for in the orthogenetic sense there is nothing Malayan, as distinct from Malay or Chinese or Indian, to revive. The city's cultural role then is to carry forward the image of a Malayan culture which at the moment barely exists. It has to provide a framework in which integration of the main cultural groups may take place, and from which eventually something Malayan will emerge; this may or may not be similar to the image of Malayan culture as it is vaguely conceived.

KUALA LUMPUR'S (DOUBTFUL) HETEROGENETIC CHARACTER

One of the principal characteristics of the heterogenetic city, as outlined by Redfield and Singer, is that it provides an environment in which local cultures are disintegrated and new integrations of mind and society are developed. It is often suggested that the Western-orientated city, in the colonial framework, is a type of cultural mixing bowl in which old folk values are destroyed and newer Western-orientated values emerge. For instance, Balandier, writing of African towns, expresses this concept when he says, 'In towns, individual cultures, after maintaining themselves for varying periods, fade into a common cultural denominator, which is at first a very meagre affair by comparison.'[9] Although this process may have occurred amongst the growing middle and upper-class elite of Kuala Lumpur between 1947 and 1957, it is doubtful if any such process occurred amongst the 'tradition-directed' dwellers who formed the majority of the city's population.[10]

Despite the rapid increase in population, the ethnic composition of Kuala Lumpur changed very little. The residential centres of the 'tradition-directed' dwellers, such as those of Chinatown and Kampong Bahru, continued to increase in population and degree of segregation, and as important centres of community institutions. The demographic structure of the various communities, although showing some evening of sex ratios, often increased in abnormality due to the drift of migrants. The political and social participation of the tradition-directed groups in the activities and administration of the city was still small.

Occupationally the basic patterns of ethnic concentration present in 1947 still persisted in 1957. While there was no lack of integration in the newer middle and upper-class groups, the manner in which the plural society functioned within a colonial framework did not force the tradition-directed groups to merge in any way. Each community functioned within its own institutional framework. For the great mass of the town's population, economic and social upgrading went on within each community. In the case of the Chinese this process occurred amongst those of the same dialect community. Thus, as Freedman pointed out, there developed an adjustment of mutual usefulness and peaceful residence among groups.[11] Whilst this facilitated commercial contacts, it did not promote a change in the cultural values of the various groups. Thus, although it is important not to regard these various racial communities as tightly closed entities in a 'Furnivallian' sense,[12] it is also significant to note that the period of rapid population growth in Kuala Lumpur between 1947 and 1957 did not bring about a 'conflict producing diversity',[13] such as occurred in Chicago in the nineteen-twenties. This 'adjustment of mutual usefulness' produced a static sociological situation, which impeded cultural change in the heterogenetic sense for the majority of the city's population.

A closer investigation of the residential, ethnic, occupational, demographic, political and social changes which occurred in the city between 1947 and 1957 supports such a thesis.

TABLE 5
NUMBERS AND PERCENTAGES OF THE MAIN ETHNIC GROUPS, KUALA LUMPUR, 1947 TO 1957

	1947		1957			Proportion of total increase (per cent)
	Number	Per cent of total Population	Number	Per cent of total Population	Rate of increase (per cent)	
Malaysians*	21,989	12·4	476,15	15·0	116·5	18·2
Chinese	111,693	63·4	195,832	62·0	75·3	59·9
Indians	31,607	17·6	53,506	16·9	69·3	15·6
Others	10,672	6·0	19,286	5·9	80·7	6·0

* Malaysians include both indigenous and immigrant Malay groups.

PATTERNS OF POPULATION INCREASE: 1947 to 1957

Although the total population of Kuala Lumpur increased by 140,000 people between 1947 and 1957, the ethnic composition of the city scarcely changed (Table 5), Kuala Lumpur remained essentially a Chinese city with small but important minority groups of Malaysians, Indians and other races.

The rates of increase of the various ethnic groups varied considerably, the Malaysians far exceeding any other racial group, with an increase of 116·5 per cent. But this represented only 18·2 per cent of the total population increase, which was dominated by the Chinese. In such a short period, it may be assumed that the large increase in the total population was not wholly due to natural increase. Almost 50 per cent of this increase (70,000) is estimated to be due to in-migration.[14] This would also make allowance for the large number of Chinese who were incorporated within the city when its boundaries were extended to include new village areas, such as Ayer Panas New Village. The majority of these immigrants were of the poorer labouring classes, many of whom moved from rural areas during the Emergency. Faced with the strangeness of the city, they tended to settle in the tradition-directed areas where they strengthened their respective communities.

There were some changes in the various dialect and language groups within the wider race categories. The Cantonese speaking group, which in 1947 was the largest Chinese dialect community, retained its dominance but showed the smallest inter-censal increase of any dialect community. This slowing down in the rate of increase may be due in part to the unbalanced sex ratio, which is heavily weighted in favour of the females.[15] In contrast to the other Chinese dialect communities, this sex ratio, far from stabilizing in the inter-censal period, continued to increase in favour of the females. This dominantly female community remains one of the most conservative elements within the Chinese community of Kuala Lumpur, fostering many traditional values brought from China, particularly religion, for as the Chinese themselves often say, 'Religion . . . is women's business'.[16] The largest increase appeared in the Hokkien community, which may indicate the extension of their occupational specializations in trade and commerce, from the economically less thriving areas of Penang and Malacca to the growing commercial 'boom' town of Kuala Lumpur. The increase of the Hakka community was almost as large as that of the Hokkiens. This was probably due to the incorporation of new villages within the boundaries of Kuala Lumpur as well as to in-migration from further afield (Table 6).

There was little change in the structure of other racial

TABLE 6

CHINESE DIALECT COMMUNITIES, KUALA LUMPUR 1947 AND 1957

	1947		*1957*		
Dialect	Number	Per cent of Total Chinese in Kuala Lumpur	Number	Per cent of Total Chinese in Kuala Lumpur	Increase (Per cent)
Cantonese	54,066	48·4	76,166	38·8	29·0
Hokkien	21,385	19·1	45,834	23·4	53·3
Hakka	20,330	18·2	43,356	22·1	53·1
Tiechiu	5,668	5·0	10,956	18·2	48·2
Hainanese	6,166	5·9	13,465	6·3	46·2

Note: These five main dialect communities made up 93 per cent of the total Chinese population in Kuala Lumpur in 1957.

communities. The Malays increased by 3 per cent to form 90 per cent of the total Malaysian community. The Tamil component of the Indian community remained dominant. Amongst the other races there was a surprising increase in the number of Europeans. The European community increased its numbers from 1,794 in 1947 to 6,645 in 1957. This was largely due to the increase of staff in European commercial houses, diplomatic personnel and the large increase in Commonwealth forces which had been fighting in the Emergency.

Thus, despite the rapid population growth of Kuala Lumpur and the large numbers of in-migrants, neither the major ethnic components of the city nor the internal dialect structure of the various communities changed to any great extent.

CHANGES IN THE PATTERN OF RESIDENCE: 1947 to 1957

Gist and Halberg's description of a city as 'veritably a "mosaic" of cultural and social worlds',[17] admirably sums up the residential patterns of Kuala Lumpur, both in 1947 and 1957. It is suprising that during a period of such rapid population growth and expansion of the city, the basic patterns of ecological segregation which existed in 1947 did not change very much. The traditional and long-established centres of the various groups; the tightly packed shophouse area of Chinatown; the area of Malay settlement—Kampong Bahru; and the areas of Indian settlement, such as Sentul and Brickfields, tended to increase their degree of ethnic segregation and remained the cultural *foci* of the majority of the social, political and economic institutions which served the more traditional elements of each of the principal racial communities. At the same time there was a growth of suburban areas on a Western pattern, particularly in the hilly areas to the west of the city, which tended to be the residential areas of the wealthy Chinese, the new political and administrative elite amongst the Malays and Indians, and the European managerial and diplomatic groups. The extension of the city's boundaries in the north and east incorporated several 'new villages', which had been established on the outskirts of the city during the Emergency. But these were dominantly Chinese, and only incorporated segregated communities on the borders of the city, which added little to the patterns of ethnic mixing within the city.

Because only limited comparable figures are available, it is impossible to support this rather generalized picture with accurate statistical data. However, it is possible to describe the location of the race groups in 1947 and again in 1957, and then choose sample regions to give some idea of ethnic change. In 1947 the traditional areas of settlement dominated the pattern of ethnic residence within the city. The Chinese, although widely spread throughout the city, tended to be concentrated in the areas of the earliest settlement, stretching from Market Square to Circular Road in the east, and through Pudu to the Sungei Besi/Cheras Road district in the south (Figure 10). Within this region there was a great variety of housing and social groups; including the densely packed shophouse areas of Chinatown and Pudu; the long lines of lower middle class apartment-type housing in Tong Shin Terrace; the mixture of squatters' houses, industrial workshops and shophouses in Sungei Besi; and the large spacious houses of the wealthy Chinese of 'Millionaire Row' in South Circular Road.

The Indians were concentrated in two areas; one to the north of the city along Ipoh Road in the Sentul district, where railway workshops had originally provided the occupational attraction; and the other in the Brickfields area where labour lines for the Public Works Department and Malayan Railways had been

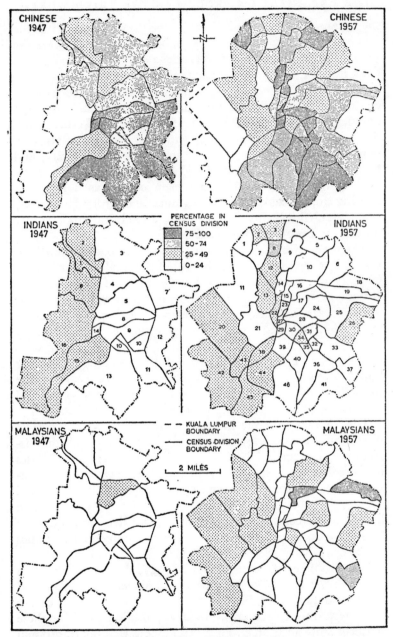

Figure 10. Distribution of ethnic groups, Kuala Lumpur, 1947 and 1957
(See page 148 for a key to these census divisions)

the original focus of settlement. The Malaysians, with the smallest percentage of the three main ethnic groups, were the most highly concentrated. Forty-six per cent of their population lived in the area known as Kampong Bahru, which lies to the north of the Klang river. This was originally a planned settlement, established by the British administration in the late eighteen-nineties, and has persisted as the main area of Malay settlement in the city.[18] The areas with the greatest mixture of population occurred on the hills to the west of the city, and between Ampang Road and Weld Road. The high land to the west of the city had originally been chosen as a high-cost housing site for colonial administrators, and, although by 1947 Malayan civil servants had begun to reside in this area, 30 per cent of the Europeans still lived there.

The other district of high-cost housing (Ampang Road/Weld Road) included many of the houses of the wealthy commercial Chinese and Europeans. One final element of the residential ecology of Kuala Lumpur, which must be mentioned, is the 'squatter settlements'. These grew up during the Japanese occupation, when an impoverished economy brought many people of the immigrant Chinese and Indian labouring class into the town in search of a living.[19] The squatters built their huts on low lying marshy flood plains in the heart of the town. The insecurity of their tenure, their low incomes and poor housing posed severe problems of administration.

Thus Kuala Lumpur in 1947 presented an almost perfect picture of a colonial town—a small group of foreign administrators and commercial officials living in large spacious houses in the hilly parts of the city, while the great mass of the population were assembled in ethnically and culturally segregated communities on the lowlands. The two social groupings had little cultural contact with each other, but lived in a phase of 'mutual adjustment' necessitated by the commercial activities of the city.

What changes had come about by 1957? As can be seen from Figure 10, the major patterns of ethnic concentration had changed only slightly, but the increase in the number of census districts and their smaller size make it possible to describe these patterns more accurately. First, it is obvious that the traditional centres of race concentration have persisted. The desire to live amongst people of similar race, language, religion and culture is one of the main factors responsible for this persistence. Probably the preference of such people to live close to their place of work is another important locational factor. In all these areas, densities have increased and there appears to be no marked movement from such areas to the middle-class housing districts. The greater detail of the distribution of race groups in Figure 10 reveals that these areas are not so homogeneous as is shown in the 1947 census. For instance, the area of Chinese settlement, stretching from Chinatown south-eastwards to Sungei Besi, is interrupted by an area of mixed population housed in government quarters. However, Kampong Bahru; Pudu, Chinatown and Sungei Besi; Sentul and Brickfields persisted as the main areas of concentration for the Malays, Chinese and Indians respectively.

The political, social and economic forces which had been operating during this period of change, leading to independence, had produced some modifications in the residential patterns of the city. An attempt had been made to solve the problem of the squatter settlements through the provision of low-cost multi-storey flats. The area between Batu Road and the Gombak River had been cleared and low-cost apartment houses erected. But the squatter settlements proliferated wherever land could be found, and the problems outlined earlier still remained. The extension of the city's boundaries had incorporated Ayer Panas New Village in the north, which added a concentration of Chinese to the pattern of the city. In the east, Dato Kramat Kampong, another concentration of Malays, was brought within the city boundary.

The ethnically more mixed middle and upper-class residential areas expanded. These can be divided into four principal groups: (i) areas of government housing, such as the Lake Gardens, Kampong Pandan and Merdeka Stadium census divisions, where racial mixing occurred because of increasing diversification in government service; (ii) wealthy residential areas, such as Kenny Hill, Ampang Road and Golf View Road, which are the chief dwelling places of European diplomats and business executives, Malayan ministers, and wealthy Chinese and Indians; (iii) middle class areas where the degree of segregation is still high, such as Pahang Road; and (iv) lower middle-class areas such as Tong Shin Terrace. The difference in housing is shown clearly in Figure 11,[20] which is a cross-section between Kenny Hill and Golf View Road. High-rental

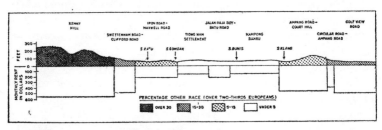

Figure 11. Vertical profile across Kuala Lumpur, relating relief, monthly rent and the concentration of Other Race groups, 1957

housing is concentrated on Kenny Hill, where rents average $500 a month, and the other race groups, of which the Europeans make up nearly two-thirds, constitute over 30 per cent of the total residents. The rental per month drops rapidly on the low-land flood plains of the Batu and Gombak rivers, and in the traditional areas of ethnic concentration of Chinese and Malaysians—Tiong Nam Settlement and Kampong Bahru, where average rents are in the vicinity of $150 per month. Rentals increase again in the Ampang Road—Court Hill—Golf View Road area to $500 per month.[21]

Thus in 1957, although the degree of mixing in these middle to upper-class areas had increased, they still included a large number of non-Malayans, and there was a sharp division between the small middle and upper-class areas, where social contacts were largely with non-Malayans, and the traditional areas of settlement on the low-lying river plains. Consequently, although Kuala Lumpur had ceased to be a colonial city the growing middle and upper class of Malayans were separated to a great extent, physically by residence, economically by wealth, and socially by choice, from the great mass of the city's population who dwelt in the tradition-directed areas where little racial merging had occurred. A comparison of the population in these three main areas in 1947 and 1957 illustrates this point

(Table 7). Thus another social division had been imposed upon the traditional racial division of the plural society, that between the new administrative and commercial elite and the tradition-bound dwellers of the city.

TABLE 7

CHANGES IN THE CONCENTRATION OF ETHNIC GROUPS IN SELECTED AREAS,
1947 TO 1975

		Population (as a percentage of the total)			
Area		Malaysian	Indian	Chinese	Others
Chinatown	1947	1·3	1·8	96·7	—
	1957	1·7	1·7	96·3	0·3
Sentul Indian	1947	7·1	37·8	44·8	10·1
	1957	11·5	34·8	44·8	8·7
Kampong Bahru	1947	49·6	3·4	45·7	1·1
	1957	50·0	3·2	45·3	1·3

CHANGES IN POPULATION STRUCTURE: 1947 to 1957

Although the changes in the pattern of residence and ethnic composition of the population of Kuala Lumpur between 1947 and 1957 were only slight, the demographic structure of the city changed considerably. All communities showed an increase in the youthful component of their age structures; they all stabilized their sex ratios and increased their fertility rates. These demographic trends seem to indicate that a population was emerging which was Malaya-born, stable and presumably more orientated towards the growth of an orthogenetic tradition. In the Chinese community, increasing youthfulness, the smaller percentages in the 30 to 45 age group and a sizeable proportion of the community in the over 45 age group (Table 8 and Figure 12) represented the dualism between the older Chinese immigrants who were born in China, and the younger Malaya-born Chinese. In 1947 the older Chinese dominated the community numerically, but by 1957 they were ageing and decreasing rapidly. Second and third generation Chinese now form almost two-thirds of the community in Kuala Lumpur.

TABLE 8
KUALA LUMPUR CHINESE, AGE STRUCTURES, 1947 TO 1957

	1947			*1957*		
Age Group	*Males (per cent)*	*Females (per cent)*	*Total Population (per cent)*	*Males (per cent)*	*Females (per cent)*	*Total Population (per cent)*
0–14	19·1	17·5	36·6	20·7	19·6	40·3
15–29	12·3	11·4	23·7	13·6	12·7	26·3
30–44	11·6	9·6	21·2	7·5	7·9	15·4
45–59	6·6	5·3	11·9	6·2	5·5	11·7
60–69	1·7	1·7	3·4	1·6	1·7	3·3

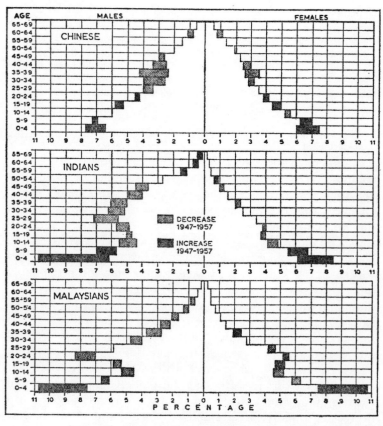

Figure 12. Age structures, Kuala Lumpur, 1947–57

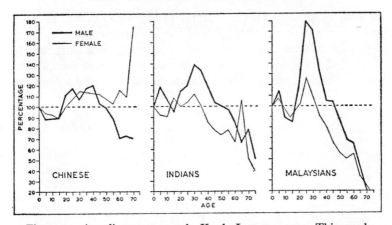

Figure 13. Age divergency graph, Kuala Lumpur, 1957. This graph
shows the percentage divergency, by race and sex, of the Kuala Lumpur
population from the same age group of the total Malayan population
by race and sex.
100 represents the total Malayan population, by race and sex, in each
age group

This dualism is to some extent modified when the age structure of the Kuala Lumpur Chinese population is compared
with that of the total Malayan Chinese population in 1957
(Figure 13). Surprisingly, the percentage below 15 is less than
the national figure, and this may be accounted for by a lower
fertility in the urban areas.[22] The Kuala Lumpur Chinese
population has a particularly large proportion in the 30 to 50
years ago bracket, which may be explained in part by the large
amount of Chinese in-migration during the period between
1947 and 1957, much of it in this age group. The sharp deviation
of females in the age groups above 50 may be explained by the
unreliability of the statistics, the longer life expectancy of
Chinese women and the predominance of Cantonese women in
the city, many of whom are in these age groups.

The sex ratio* of the Kuala Lumpur Chinese has stabilized
at a much faster rate than that of the total Malayan Chinese
population, but when this gross pattern of sex for the whole
Kuala Lumpur Chinese is broken down according to dialect

---

* Throughout this paper sex ratio is defined as the number of males per 100
females.

communities the pattern changes (Table 9). The sex ratio in every case, with the exception of the Hainanese community, is less well balanced than the national figure. This is particularly true of the Cantonese, amongst whom the female component has increased considerably, and who unquestionably weight the

TABLE 9

MAJOR CHINESE DIALECT COMMUNITIES (KUALA LUMPUR), SEX RATIOS, 1947 TO 1957

Dialect	1947	1957
Cantonese	92·8	89·9
Hokkien	123·1	114·5
Tiechiu	136·0	117·7
Hakka	116·5	106·5
Hainanese	172·2	132·4
Kuala Lumpur (Total Chinese)	111·0	103·0
Malaya (Total Chinese)	121·0	107·9

total Chinese sex ratios to give a greater appearance of normality than really exists.

The second largest alien community in the city, the Indians, retained their immigrant characteristics to a high degree. Although the age structure showed an increasing youthfulness (Table 10, and Figure 12), the age groups above 15 remained

TABLE 10

KUALA LUMPUR INDIANS, AGE STRUCTURES, 1947 TO 1957

Age Group	1947			1957		
	Males (per cent)	Females (per cent)	Total Population (per cent)	Males (per cent)	Females (per cent)	Total Population (per cent)
0–14	17·4	16·4	33·8	22·2	19·4	41·6
15–29	17·6	11·3	28·9	15·3	11·1	26·4
30–44	17·1	6·3	23·4	14·5	6·2	20·7
45–59	8·4	2·0	10·4	8·2	2·2	10·4
60–69	0·7	0·4	1·1	1·0	0·4	1·4

heavily weighted in favour of the males. This dominance of males is further accentuated when the Kuala Lumpur Indian population is compared with the total Malayan Indian population (Figure 13), which clearly shows the excess of males in the Kuala Lumpur population. The sex ratio reveals the same feature (Table 11). That the Indian community in Kuala

TABLE 11
KUALA LUMPUR INDIANS, SEX RATIOS, 1947 TO 1957

	1947	1957
Kuala Lumpur	166·2	149·1
Total Malaya	145·6	133·9

Lumpur has retained many of its immigrant characteristics is a feature which distinguishes it demographically from the other racial groups.

The Malaysian pyramid reflects in-migration to the largest degree. Although the largest percentage of the Malaysians are in the youthful age group (Table 12, Figure 12), it is the 20 to

TABLE 12
KUALA LUMPUR MALAYSIANS, AGE STRUCTURES, 1947 TO 1957

Age Group	1947			1957		
	Males (per cent)	Females (per cent)	Total Population (per cent)	Males (per cent)	Females (per cent)	Total Population (per cent)
0–14	18·7	19·4	38·1	21·4	21·6	43·0
15–29	19·5	14·9	34·4	17·9	14·9	32·8
30–44	10·6	6·7	17·3	9·0	6·6	15·6
45–59	3·8	2·4	6·2	2·4	2·2	4·6
60–69	0·7	0·7	1·4	1·4	0·4	1·8

30 years age group that stands out most (Figure 13). This age group is heavily weighted in favour of males, reflecting the male-dominated character of Malaysian migration into the city. This weights the sex ratio of the entire Malaysian community in favour of males, whereas that for the whole of Malaya shows a predominance of females. The chief attractions of the city for the Malaysian males are the increasing number of occupational opportunities in the civil service, the police and the armed services. Lack of occupational opportunities for women, and social pressure to remain in the kampong, are the principal reasons why there is no comparable migration of Malaysian females. The other striking feature of the Malaysian age pyramid is the small percentage in the older age groups. This may

be explained by two factors. First, the desire of the urban Malaysians to retire to their kampongs. Secondly, Malaysians are comparatively recent migrants to the city, and there has been insufficient time for the old-age component of the population to build up (Table 13).

TABLE 13
KUALA LUMPUR MALAYSIANS, SEX RATIOS, 1947 TO 1957

	1947	*1957*
Kuala Lumpur	132·7	113·3
Total Malaya	99·0	98·6

The population of Kuala Lumpur may be divided into three broad age groupings. The largest is the youthful group below 21, which includes more than 50 per cent of the city's total population. Although their importance in the city's power hierarchy and institutions is as yet small, it is to this group that the new cultural values of Malayan nationhood must be applied. The success of Kuala Lumpur's transition to an orthogenetic city will depend, to a great extent, upon the reaction of this group. The second group, which accounts for 30 to 35 per cent of the city's population, includes those between 21 and 45 years of age. It is in this age group, which is male dominated, that the majority of the new migrants to the city are found. It is an open question as to how quickly an orthogenetic attitude can be built up in these new residents, who appear to be concerned only with solving their own social problems, and with adjustment to city life. Finally, there are those of the older age groups who, although possessing considerable power particularly in the immigrant communities, are numerically small and decreasing.

OCCUPATIONAL MOBILITY: 1947 to 1957

Although Furnivall's description of the economic structure of plural societies in Southeast Asia, as characterized by a high degree of occupational specialization on the part of the different race groups and a sharp economic cleavage in the incomes of indigenous and immigrant groups, must undergo considerable modification when it is applied to the urban environment, it serves as a useful summing up of the occupational characteristics of Kuala Lumpur in 1947. This pattern had changed little by 1957. The tendency for each of the major ethnic groups to concentrate in particular occupations (the Chinese in commerce, manufacturing and domestic services; the Indians in transport and communications; and the Malaysians in administration, the police force and the armed services), imposes an additional economic cleavage on the cultural and ethnic divisions in the city, making the task of imposing an orthogenetic cultural role doubly difficult. Before any orthogenetic tradition, based on an integrated Malayan society, can be built up there must be occupational mixing. This did not occur to any great extent in Kuala Lumpur between 1947 and 1957.

In 1947, over two-thirds of the employed Chinese in Kuala Lumpur were engaged in the manufacturing and commercial and financial industrial sectors. In both of these groups they formed over 70 per cent of the employment (Table 14). Within

TABLE 14
ETHNIC PROPORTIONS IN INDUSTRY, 1947 AND 1957
(Figures are percentages)

	Malaysians		Chinese		Indians		Others	
	1947	*1957*	*1947*	*1957*	*1947*	*1957*	*1947*	*1957*
Manufacturing	11·8	10·5	73·0	73·1	13·4	15·0	1·5	1·1
Transport and Communications	16·4	23·7	43·7	36·9	33·6	32·1	6·1	7·2
Commerce and Finance	4·9	7·6	75·0	69·4	18·2	20·0	1·7	2·9
Public Administration and Defence	31·7	38·7	22·5	24·4	35·7	19·0	9·9	17·8
Professions and Entertainment	22·8	17·8	54·4	55·6	17·4	21·9	5·5	4·5
Personal Services	10·3	10·4	64·4	69·0	24·2	19·1	0·9	1·6

these two sectors the majority were employed in small-scale industries such as car repairing, and retail occupations such as hawking, and as shop proprietors and salesman. The Chinese also formed a high proportion of those employed in personal services (64 per cent), of which the majority were female domestic servants. Their lowest concentration was in public administration and defence within the professional occupational groupings. The Chinese formed the majority in the medical and law professions.

On the other hand, the Malaysians were most heavily concentrated in the public administration and defence sector; particularly in government service and the police and armed forces. As yet few had entered the professions. For instance, there were only three Malaysian doctors as compared with 163 Chinese. In the other occupations the Malaysians were generally at the bottom of the occupational ladder, in unskilled work such as office peons and hawkers. The other race groups, of whom the majority were Europeans, were also highly concentrated in the professional, administrative and defence sectors, as might be expected within the framework of the colonial administration. Finally, the Indians too showed a tendency to concentrate in this group, but the majority were engaged in public works, and a large number were employed by the railway.

This pattern of occupational concentration shows a sharp division between the Chinese, who controlled the commercial activities of the city, and the Malaysians and Europeans, who were dominant in the political and administrative sectors.

Despite the rapid increase of population between 1947 and 1957, the changes in this pattern of occupational concentration were only slight. The Chinese remained the dominant element in the manufacturing industries, which showed the greatest increase in the numbers employed of any industrial sector in the city. The Malaysians showed an increasing tendency to concentrate in public administration and defence, which reflects the increasing numbers of Malaysians entering the civil service and the very large-scale recruitment of Malaysians into the army and the police force. The surprising increase, by 1957, of other races in public administration and defence was principally the result of the large influx of Commonwealth Forces, brought in to fight the Communist terrorists and hasten the end of the Emergency.

There were, however, some changes. The percentage of Chinese engaged in commerce and finance decreased with the increase in the percentage of Indians and other races in this occupation. The Malaysians, who did not possess the skills or the necessary capital, despite the fact that they increased their numbers in this sector, increased their percentage of employment only slightly.

The Chinese increased in number in public administration, professional and defence groups of occupations, mainly because of the increasing number in the professional sector. They still formed a very small percentage of the total employed personnel in the civil service, the police and armed forces. But in general the occupational patterns of 1947 persisted and there was little occupational mixing.

The occupational differences are reflected in the income patterns of the three principal communities (Table 15). The

TABLE 15

FEDERATION OF MALAYA, URBAN INCOMES, 1947 TO 1957

Income per Month (in Malayan $)	Chinese	Malaysian	Indian
1– 150	24·5	33·0	45·0
150– 300	41·5	45·0	33·0
300– 500	21·7	14·8	13·6
500–1000	12·3	7·2	8·4

concentration of Chinese in the commercial and financial occupations is reflected in their much higher incomes. Over 34 per cent of the urban Chinese earned more than $300 per month, while only 22 per cent of the Malaysians and Indians earned more than this amount. There was, however, an interesting division in the lower incomes between the three race groups. Forty-five per cent of the Malaysians earned between $150 and $300 per month, which probably reflects their concentration in commerce, government administration, the police and the armed forces, whose salaries fall predominantly in this bracket. The Indians had the largest percentage in the lowest income bracket, indicating their concentration in the unskilled and poorly paid semi-skilled jobs. Thus the occupational concentrations of the particular extra groups are reflected in the income pattern of the city, which further serve to create divisions between the various communities.

THE GROWTH OF POLITICS: 1947 to 1961

Internal political development in Kuala Lumpur was slow, despite the major political events of the decade prior to 1957, such as the rapid movement of Malaya towards independence, the formation of the major political parties and the first nation-wide elections in 1954. Before Kuala Lumpur became a Municipality in 1948, the majority of the town councillors were nominated, either by the Sultan or by various communal organizations, such as the Chinese Chamber of Commerce, the European Chamber of Commerce, the Ceylonese Association, and the Committee of the Malay Settlement. The town councillors tended to come from the middle and upper classes, and the mass of the tradition-directed dwellers showed little concern for politics. This lack of political interest is frequently commented upon in the Town Commissioners' Reports. 'The question of elections has not yet come to the fore. The apathy and lack of civil sense on the part of the general public are perhaps the inevitable result of fifty years of "benevolent bureaucracy" wielded by the State Department.'[23]

With the creation of the Municipality in 1948, provision was made for the election of two-thirds of the councillors by popular ballot. The remaining one-third were to be nominated by the Resident Commissioner, the latter's nominees representing those sections of the community which failed to obtain representation by ballot.[24] The electoral franchise was modelled on the municipal areas of England, imposing required qualifications on the electorate, such as residential property ownership and minimum rents of $30 a month. This meant that a considerable portion of the town's population, particularly the squatters and cubicle-dwellers of Chinatown, were cut off from political participation. It is hardly surprising that they evinced little interest in politics or administration.

However, local elections based on this electoral formula were not held until 1952, when twelve of the twenty councillors were elected on this rather limited franchise. At this time, although municipal political participation was very slow and hardly represented the hopes of the British administration that it would be the 'nursery of local self government', there was a rapid movement towards the development of national self-government on a parliamentary model. The nation-wide elections of 1954 saw the first established parties putting up candidates in the two parliamentary districts which made up Kuala Lumpur.

The Alliance Party (an alliance of the Malayan Chinese Association, the United Malay Organization and the Indian Congress with a party platform of independence and a united Malaya) nominated two Chinese candidates for the Kuala Lumpur seats and emerged an easy winner, gaining 64·4 per cent of the votes.[25] Its opposition came mainly from the Party Negara, under the leadership of Dato Onn bin Jaafar and an Independent candidate. At this time the left wing parties were poorly organized, and the Labour Party candidate polled a very low number of votes.

It was not until after 1957 that political activity on a national basis began to build up in the city. Particularly important was the growth of the Socialist Front, whose policies appealed to the immigrant proletarian community. In 1954 the left wing parties had virtually no foothold in the city. But in the State elections of 1959 the Socialist Front polled 34 per cent of the total vote in the eight constituencies which formed part of the city, though they only won two of the seats. Their strongest support came from the areas of the city which have been described as the 'immigrant traditional areas', such as Sentul, and Bukit Nanas including Chinatown. The Alliance Party gained one of these 'traditional areas', Kampong Bahru, mainly because of its reliance upon the Malay vote. The Socialist Front further increased its strength in the parliamentary elections winning three of the four Kuala Lumpur seats, and gaining 44 per cent of the votes cast in the area. However, the political apathy, mentioned earlier, persisted. Only 65 per cent of those entitled to vote did so, compared with the national figure of 73 per cent.[26]

The increasing strength of the opposition left wing party, and its support from the traditional elements of the city, has not only further divided the tradition-directed dwellers of the city from the new Malayan administrative and commercial elite, but it has posed a fundamental dilemma to this class, who are trying to build up an orthogenetic tradition. How, for instance, can Kuala Lumpur, the federal capital, focus and disseminating point of the new Malayan culture, be administered by a political party which is opposed in many aspects of its policy to the Federal Government? The solution to this problem has been to suspend local authority elections indefinitely in the city. Thus in 1961, when local authority elections were held throughout Malaya, no elections were held in the local authority area of Kuala Lumpur. Whether such an attempt to stultify political developments within the city will in fact allow a breathing space in which the orthogenetic tradition can be established remains to be seen.

THE DIFFICULTY OF CREATING AN ORTHOGENETIC ROLE FOR KUALA LUMPUR

The conclusions of this discussion support the rather pessimistic introductory note of Redfield and Singer, regarding the difficulties of creating an orthogenetic role for a city with a colonial heritage. It has been suggested that this problem is doubly difficult in Kuala Lumpur because of the complex ethnic, social, demographic, economic and political divisions which exist in the city. If Kuala Lumpur had possessed the important heterogenetic characteristic of an environment in which local cultures were disintegrated and new integrations of mind and society appeared, this would have provided a situation extremely favourable to the creation of an orthogenetic role. Although this occurred in the small and racially mixed Malayan middle class of political leaders, administrators and professional men, for the vast majority of the city's inhabitants no such integration occurred. The tradition-directed residential centres persisted, and occupational specialization remained. Politically, the support of the inhabitants of the tradition-directed residential centres moved away from the policy makers of the orthogenetic tradition, and culturally the two groups remained separate. Thus, between 1947 and 1957 there was no move by the mass of the population to a position where they could accept the orthogenetic tradition.

Almost as great a problem was the absence of a Malayan orthogenetic tradition to revive. Unlike other colonial countries, particularly India, there was no historical tradition of a national culture in Malaya; but simply a diverse collection of Malay, Chinese, Indonesian and Indian folk cultures. Thus an orthogenetic cultural role had to be created. There was little doubt as to what it was desired to create—a Malayan tradition with Malayan, rather than Chinese or Malay, cultural values. There was, however, great difficulty in formulating a policy which would create such a set of cultural values. Thus a policy of cultural compromise, which seems to be a graft of Malay culture onto the other cultural elements of Malaya, was evolved. Such a policy was piecemeal, and showed little understanding of the richness of cultural diversity in the country. In addition, because it was made by a political elite who had become secularized and had lost contact with the more traditional elements of their own cultures, it failed to take into account the cultural resilience of these groups. It is rather like trying to build a dam across a large river without engineering equipment or constructional plans. The results might well be disastrous!

Such a conclusion may be altogether too pessimistic, because in reality there was little alternative to such a policy. Any policy which imposes one culture at the expense of another is bound to meet with disaster. Today the educational and political institutions which are expected to disseminate the ideas of a united Malayan culture are growing rapidly in Kuala Lumpur; for example—the University of Malaya, the National Training College, the Language Institute, the Federal Government Departments and the Federal Government itself. Although these institutions are important in the establishment of the orthogenetic tradition, the divided character of the city must change if it is to be a truly representative orthogenetic city. Now that the static conditions of the post-war colonial period have gone, perhaps the period of rapid urban development, which Kuala Lumpur is now undergoing, will create flexible conditions of mixing and social and occupational upgrading. This seems to be the first requisite for such a change. The second requirement is a rapid education of the youthful population in Malayan values. If these two requirements are realized, it may well be that the greater cultural consciousness necessary to effect Kuala Lumpur's successful transition to an orthogenetic city will have been achieved.

NOTES

1. Robert Redfield and Milton B. Singer, 'The Cultural Role of Cities', *Economic Development and Cultural Change*, 3, 1, October, 1954, p. 59
2. Ibid., pp. 53–73

3. Concepts of culture are almost as numerous as definitions of geography, but for the purposes of this paper culture is defined as comprising the inherited sets of techniques, value systems and social structure which determine the behaviour patterns of a society.

4. Gunnar Myrdal, *Value in Social Theory—A Selection of Essays on Methodology*, London, 1958, p. 52

5. J. M. Gullick, 'Kuala Lumpur, 1880–1895', *Journal of the Malayan Branch of the Royal Asiatic Society*, 28, 172, p. 8

6. In the context of this paper 'nation building' does not imply the physical merging of ethnic groups, but rather the attempt to replace the communal systems of thinking with a Malayan set of values and beliefs. In particular this would be concerned with building up a belief in one's country before one's ethnic community. In simple terms it means the building of national belief before a communal one. At the same time it is based on a policy which recognizes that the only hope of accomplishing such a task quickly is by breaking down the communal barriers and cultural values of the various ethnic groups.

7. For a discussion of the growth of this middle class in the developing world see: International Institute of Differing Civilizations, *Development of a Middle Class in Tropical and Sub-tropical countries*, Brussels, 1956, and in particular Francis G. Carnell's essay entitled 'The development of the Middle Class in Burma, Thailand and Malaya', pp. 271–9

8. 'Cultural pluralism' as defined by Kiser, implies that the persistence of the cultural patterns of the different races is not opposed to the growth of a belief in an unified Malaya, in addition to a pride in the individual's own community. See Clyde V. Kiser, 'Cultural Pluralism' in Joseph J. Spengler and Otis Dudley Duncan (eds.), *Demographic Analysis*, Glencoe, Illinois, 1956, pp. 307–20

9. G. Balandier, 'Urbanism in West and Central Africa: the scope and aims of research', U.N.E.S.C.O., *Social Implications of Industrialization and Urbanization in Africa South of the Sahara*, Paris, 1956, p. 496

10. 'Tradition-directed' is defined as those inhabitants of the city among whom folk values and communal attitudes still persist, as distinct from the Westernized middle and upper classes who have broken from their traditional background. Just as Redfield has constructed a 'conceptual model' of 'peasant society' distinct with the wider context of agricultural society, it is possible to construct a similar model for different societies within the urban environment.

11. Maurice Freedman, 'The Growth of a Plural Society in Malaya', *Pacific Affairs*, XXXIII, 2, June, 1960, pp. 158–68

12. See J. S. Furnivall, *Netherlands India, A study of Plural Economy*, Cambridge, 1939

13. See William L. Kolb, 'The Social Structure and Function of Cities', *Economic Development and Cultural Change*, 3, 1, October, 1954, pp. 30–47

14. This estimate is based on a calculated 3 per cent natural increase, which would mean a 30 per cent increase in the city's population over the ten-year period. As the population increased by almost 80 per cent, much of the remaining increase must have been due to in-migration as

well as boundary expansion. Since it is impossible to calculate the proportion of the population increase contributed by boundary increase we will assume that in-migration has accounted for 50 per cent of the increase.

15. The dominance of Cantonese women is the result of the large influx of female immigrants between 1933 and 1938, when the Alien's Ordinance, which restricted male labour coincided with the failure of the silk industry in China. Many women left their families and tried to find employment in Malaya. See Siew Nim Chee, 'Labour and Tin Mining in Malaya' in T. H. Silcock, *Readings in Malayan Economics*, Singapore, 1961, pp. 404–39

16. Maurice Freedman, *Chinese Family and Marriage in Singapore*, London, 1957, p. 45

17. N. P. Gist and W. Halberg, *Urban Society*, p. 137

18. See John Hands, 'Malay Agricultural Settlement, Kuala Lumpur. A Short History', *The Malayan Historical Journal*, 2, 2, December, 1955, pp. 146–62

19. W. J. Bennet, 'Kuala Lumpur: A town in the Equatorial Lowlands', *Tijdschrift voor Economische en Sociale Geografie*, 12, December, 1961, p. 328

20. This technique of showing ethnic distribution in relation to the rental rates of housing was adapted from that used in L. Kuper, H. Watts, and R. Davies, *Durban. A Study in Racial Ecology*, London, 1958

21. These rental figures were provided by the Municipal Valuation Department, Kuala Lumpur.

22. See T. E. Smith, *Population Growth in Malaya*, London, 1952

23. *Annual Report of the Kuala Lumpur Municipality for the Year 1948*, Kuala Lumpur, 1949, pp. 2–3

24. *Report of the Committee appointed to consider the Establishment of a Municipality in Kuala Lumpur*, Kuala Lumpur, 1947, p. 3

25. T. E. Smith, *Report on the First Election of Members to the Legislative Council of the Federation of Malaya*, Kuala Lumpur, 1955, p. 71

26. Election Commission, *Report on the Parliamentary and State Elections, 1959*, Kuala Lumpur, 1960. For an anlysis of the elections see T. G. McGee, 'The 1959 Elections in Malaya. A Case Study in Electoral Geography', *The Journal of Tropical Geography*, 16, 1962, pp. 70–99

AUTHOR'S NOTE: As this paper was written in 1962 I have the used terms which were used at that time to describe the various races of Malaya. Thus 'Malaysian' may be equated with Malay while 'Malayan' means any inhabitant of any race who was resident in the Malayan peninsula.

APPENDIX

Key to the location of census divisions in Kuala Lumpur

1947

1.	Ipoh Road	9.	Pudu Road
2.	Sentul	10.	Loke Yew Road—Cheras Road
3.	Prince's Road—Pahang Road		
4.	Jalan Rajah Bot—Kampong Bahru	11.	Sungei Besi Road—Cheras Road
5.	Batu Road—Ampang Road—Circular Road	12.	Jalan Kampong Padan
		13.	Sungei Besi Road
6.	Swettenham Road—Batu Road	14.	Petaling Street—Foch Avenue
		15.	Brickfields Road—Bungsar Road
7.	Circular Road—Ampang Road		
8.	Bukit Bintang Road	16.	Lake Gardens

1957

1.	Segabut Road	25.	Golf View Road
2.	4th Mile Ipoh Road	26.	Kampong Pandan Village
3.	Sentul Pasar	27.	Embankment/Foch Avenue
4.	Gomback/Klang Gates	28.	Tong Shin Terrace.
5.	Ayer Panas Village	29.	Petaling Street/Foch Avenue
6.	Gurney Road	30.	Merdeka Stadium
7.	Ipoh Road/Sentul Workshop	31.	Pudu/Jalan Brunei
8.	New Area Road	32.	Pudu Road/Pasir Road
9.	Pahang Road	33.	Cheras Road/Kampong Pandan
10.	Gurney Road/Hospital		
11.	Kenny Hill	34.	Loke Yew Road/Shaw Road
12.	Ipoh Road/Maxwell Road	35.	Loke Yew Road/San Peng Road
13.	Swettenham/Clifford Roads		
14.	Tiong Nam Settlement	36.	Sungei Besi Road/Cheras Road
15.	Jalan Rajah Bot/Batu Road	37.	Old Cheras Road
16.	Kampong Bahru	38.	Brickfields
17.	Ampang Road/Court Hill	39.	Birch Road/Petaling Hill
18.	Dato Kramat Kampong	40.	Sungei Besi/Sanpeng Roads
19.	Circular Road/Ampang Road	41.	Cheras Road/Salak South
20.	Bungsar Estate	42.	Pantai
21.	Lake Gardens	43.	Bungsar Road
22.	Victory Avenue/Coliseum	44.	Lornie Road/Cemetery
23.	Batu Lane/Campbell Road	45.	Klang Road
24.	Ampang Road/Parry Road	46.	R.A.F. Station

☆ 6 ☆

Malays in Kuala Lumpur City:
An Investigation of one Aspect of the
Process of Urbanization—Occupational
Mobility

In modern stratified urban communities the tendency to change one's social position is more marked than in small-scale societies. Individuals seek to improve their social position by moving to communities where opportunities are prevalent and by changing their occupation for one which provides increased economic power or confers more prestige.[1]

INTRODUCTION

THE ASSERTION that the cities of the industrialized Western world provide an environment which is favourable to occupational and social mobility of the city populations has been widely accepted.[2] Seymour Lipset has suggested three main reasons for this prevalence of social and occupational mobility. First, 'the greater degree of specialization and a more complex division of labour . . .' in the cities offers more positions and thus, 'a greater likelihood, on a chance or random basis alone . . .' of occupational moves. Secondly, the growth of cities in the Western world has generally been associated with expanding employment opportunities and thus there have generally been new positions to be occupied in the cities. Thirdly, the lower fertility rates of the cities, compared to the countryside, has allowed migration to the urban areas to 'fill the gaps created by the low birth rates'. In addition, the lower reproduction rates of the upper socio-economic strata has permitted upward mobility.[3]

The existence of these favourable processes has led to a pattern of occupational mobility in these cities which is described by Lipset as follows:

> The cycle in which immigrants or migrants into large cities take over the lower-status position while the native urbanites move up in the occupation structure has been one of the most important processes underlying social mobility ever since these cities began to expand rapidly. It is this cycle which gives to cities their character of great mobility and ever present change. Of those persons born and raised in cities, some are socially mobile and some, of course, are not. But they all tend to stay in the city (although they frequently move from one urban centre to another). On the other hand, rural and small-town dwellers, if they move out of their parental status, are most likely to do so in a large city—while their more stable neighbors remain in their place of origin.[4]

It is obvious that doubts may be expressed concerning the universal application of this model to all Western societies. The processes favourable to this pattern of occupational mobility have clearly varied a great deal from Western society to society, among regions of particular countries and from city to city. Moreover, the prospects of occupational mobility have been unevenly distributed among the migrant groups who have moved to the various cities. For instance, it is clear that the prospects of occupational mobility for the rural Negro entering the cities of the southern United States are much less than those of the white migrant.[5] Occupational mobility has also been hindered in some Western cities by the tendency for some minority groups to concentrate in some relatively low-status occupations for long periods, because they find them financially rewarding, despite the lack of obvious barriers to upward occupational mobility in the host society.[6] These examples, however, refer to the lack of opportunities of occupational mobility for minority groups in the city and do not invalidate the argument that for the majority of the city populations, upward mobility is possible and prevalent.[7]

The purpose of this paper is to investigate the occupational mobility of one group in a Third World city, in order to ascertain whether this 'rags to riches' cycle of occupational mobility is being repeated. First, however, it is necessary to consider whether the processes favourable to occupational mobility, already enumerated by Lipset, are operating in the Third World cities.[8]

BARRIERS TO OCCUPATIONAL MOBILITY—in the Third World Cities

The vastly different circumstances of urbanization in the Third World have created conditions in which the processes favourable to occupational mobility are far less than those existing in the Western city. To take Lipset's first assertion that the complex division of labour offers more positions and thus a greater likelihood of occupational mobility, in *a priori* terms there can be little debate with this proposition. However, when the immigrant groups which occupied various sectors of the labour force during the colonial period continue to dominate these sectors in the post-Independence period, the number of positions available to the largely indigenous rural migrants moving into the cities are limited. The consolidation of various ethnic groups within particular occupational niches in the cities of the Third World has left a major barrier to occupational mobility in the post-Independence period.[9]

The second favourable process which emphasized the boost that expanding employment opportunities gave to occupational mobility in the Western cities is certainly not being repeated in all Third World cities. Whereas in the West, expanding employment opportunities were intimately bound up with the growth of industrialization and improvements in agriculture which freed the agricultural labour force for its move to the cities, in many of the Third World countries the situation is radically different. In these areas the slowness of industrialization and the inability to bring about an agricultural revolution comparable to that of Western countries has produced a situation in which employment opportunities are not sufficient to absorb the rural migrants being pushed to the cities by the lack of employment and other problems in the rural areas. Thus many cities of the Third World, swamped by the influx of rural migrants came to 'reflect the problems of the nation at large, problems arising largely from low productivity and mass poverty'.[10] The situation is one of economic stagnation unfavourable to occupational mobility.[11]

The very different demographic circumstances of many of the Third World countries must also be considered. Lipset emphasizes the significance of the lower fertility rates of the Western cities (as compared to the countryside) which allowed migration to the urban areas to fill the occupational vacancies and to encourage occupational mobility. It would appear that these demographic patterns are not being repeated in Third World countries, for Davis has shown that many of the cities of the Third World are experiencing much higher rates of natural increase than their Western counterparts at similar periods of growth (largely due to lower mortality rates) which means that natural increase makes up a larger component of the cities' numerical growth and limits occupational opportunities for the migrants.[12]

Thus it can be argued that these processes, favourable to occupational mobility, are not being repeated in all Third World cities, making the barriers to occupational mobility considerable. The implications of this conclusion as they apply to this study of Malays' occupational mobility in Kuala Lumpur will become more obvious in the later sections. Before discussing the patterns of Malay occupational mobility, it is necessary to define the characteristics of the city in which Malays are employed and some of the features of the Malay community.

KUALA LUMPUR—A 'Central City'

In the introduction the point was made that the patterns of occupational mobility would be affected not only by the general processes already discussed, but also by the character and function of each city. Since cities are not identical, the pattern of occupational mobility will clearly vary from city to city. Furthermore, a city's functions and character change through time. Some of the inhabitants of contemporary Kuala Lumpur have lived there during three distinct periods of political administration (excluding the period of Japanese control), during which time the character and functions of the city changed considerably.

Despite these changes in political control, it can be claimed that except for the first forty years when Kuala Lumpur was 'a raw and rumbustious' Chinese mining encampment, the major theme in the history of Kuala Lumpur has been the continuing emphasis upon its role as a 'central city', a city which is the political and cultural centre of its country, and which performs many of the central economic functions of the country.[13] From its inception as the administrative centre of the British in the Federated Malay States in the 1890s, Kuala Lumpur's history has recorded the increasing importance of these functions. This is not to deny its growth as a transport centre, or the significance of the rapid grafting of commercial functions on to the dominantly Chinese city, which occurred with the growth of European tin-mining and rubber estates in the early part of the twentieth century. Accompanying this growth of commercial activity in the city was a considerable increase in the city population—from 18,000 in 1891 to 175,000 in 1947. Throughout this period the city remained essentially an administrative and commercial centre—a colonial city ruled by Europeans, dominated numerically by the immigrant Chinese and Indians while the indigenous Malays, except for the Malay aristocrats who cooperated with the European rulers, remained marginal participants.[14]

The period of the Japanese invasion in the early 1940s disrupted the structure of political power, but did little to change the ethnic composition of the city or its functions. The reassertion of British control, the failure of the attempt to set up the Malayan Union and the creation of the Federation of Malaya in 1948, with Kuala Lumpur as its capital, led to a further concentration of administrative and commercial activities in the city. There was also a period of rapid devolution towards independence and of political instability associated with the Communist revolt. The 1955 elections saw the victory of the Malay-dominated Alliance Party to the newly-created House of Representatives in Kuala Lumpur, furthering the trend to centralize political control in the city. The rapid onset of independence precipitated the movement of civil servants, police and army personnel from other states to the capital.[15]

Finally, with the independence of Malaya in August 1957, the city assumed the role of capital of the independent state of Malaya and since that date, capital of a wider grouping of territories, the Federation of Malaysia. This transition from its colonial status to independence has involved the city's assuming a new role as the central disseminating point of Malayan (and later Malaysian) national culture, further increasing its central administrative and political functions. The institutions which train the cadres of the new nation are now concentrated in the city—the university, the training and technical colleges and the army and police training establishments.[16] In addition, the growing rift between Singapore and Kuala Lumpur has led many commercial firms (already located in Singapore) to establish new offices in the capital of the new nation.[17] Thus the administrative and commercial functions of the city established during the colonial period have been accentuated in the period of post-independence.

THE POSITION OF THE MALAY COMMUNITY

The demographic, occupational and social patterns of the Malay community[18] in Kuala Lumpur are closely interwoven with this theme of the increasing importance of Kuala Lumpur as a 'central city'. Indeed an understanding of this relationship is fundamental to the patterns of occupational mobility, which will be discussed in the next section. On the one hand the functions of the city offer certain occupational opportunities. On the other, such occupational opportunities have to be perceived and desired by a group or individual seeking employment. Occupational aspirations are clearly affected by a multitude of factors among which education, age and sex are probably the most important. But in a plural society such as Malaya where each ethnic group's position in the socio-economic structure had been consolidated to such a point during the colonial period that it would take a considerable effort of either group or individual will to break out of this position, the problem posed by this situation to occupational mobility is of utmost significance. It is therefore important to discuss briefly the historical position of the Malay community in Kuala Lumpur city and in the wider context of the Malayan society.

The basic theme in the history of the Malays in Kuala Lumpur city has been the contrast between their increasing political power and their failure to penetrate those occupational sectors which would give them economic power. The increasing political strength of the Malay group both within the city and on a wider nation-wide scale has been the principal process incorporating the Malay in the city and placing him occupationally, but it has been accompanied by no similar increase in economic strength.

During the colonial period the Malays remained essentially marginal participants in the city. Numerically they were the smallest of the three main ethnic groups (see Table 16) and

TABLE 16

KUALA LUMPUR TOWN—ETHNIC COMPOSITION, 1891–1947

		Malays	Chinese	Indians	Others	Total Population
1891	%	12·2	73·2	12·4	2·0	99·8
	No.	2,333	13,927	2,367	393	19,020
1911	%	9·0	66·6	19·4	4·8	99·8
	No.	4,226	31,152	9,068	2,272	46,718
1931	%	9·6	60·9	22·7	6·6	99·8
	No.	10,769	67,929	25,342	7,378	111,418
1947	%	12·4	63·4	17·9	6·0	99·7
	No.	21,989	111,693	31,607	10,672	175,961

while their rates of increase (see Table 17) were generally higher than the other ethnic groups during the period, they were not sufficient to change their proportion of the total Kuala Lumpur population markedly. Ecologically the community was divided between the Malay reserve of Kampong Bahru and a series of peri-urban kampongs which fringed the city; although there were a small number of Malays living in ethnically mixed government quarters. Occupationally the Malays were engaged largely in service industries such as

TABLE 17

KUALA LUMPUR TOWN—MALAYS AND TOTAL POPULATION INCREASE, 1891–1947

	Malays	Total Population
1891–1901	+ 60%	+ 70%
1901–1911	+ 13%	+ 44%
1911–1921	+ 73%	+ 72%
1921–1931	+ 47%	+ 38%
1931–1947	+ 104%	+ 58%

gardening, driving, low government and white-collar clerical occupations, police and army. Many of the inhabitants of the peri-urban kampongs grew fruit and vegetables for the Kuala Lumpur market. Politically the power of the Malay was slight; while some of the traditional leaders sat on councils with the British administrators, they generally did little more than approve colonial decisions.[19] Socially the community was tight-knit, although there were social divisions between aristocrat and commoner, as well as between the Indonesian migrants and the indigenous Malays. Oral interviews indicate considerable contact between the peri-urban kampongs and the true urban Malays, mainly on religious occasions and at the weekly Sunday market held in Kampong Bahru. The Islamic religion practised by the Malays acted as an important unifying factor in the community in addition to providing an institutional framework through such groups as *surau* committees for community contact and interchange. Throughout the colonial period the Malay community can be said to have been largely marginal participants in the city's structure. The colonial rulers were content, whether by design or accident, to regard the Malay as largely a rural dweller, ill-equipped to cope with the urban environment.[20]

The ten years, 1947–57, following the defeat of the Japanese and the reassertion of British control saw a rapid increase in the number of Malays in the city as well as an increase in their proportion of the total Kuala Lumpur population (see Table 18). This had a considerable effect on the location of the Malays throughout the city for a shortage of housing, particularly in Kampong Bahru, forced many into squatter settlements within

TABLE 18
Numbers and Percentages of the Main Ethnic Groups—Kuala Lumpur, 1947–1957

	No.	% of Total Population	No.	% of Total Population	Rate of Increase (%)	Proportion of Total Increase (%)
Malays	21,989	12·4	47,615	15·0	116·5	18·2
Chinese	111,693	63·4	195,832	62·0	75·3	59·9
Indians	31,607	17·6	53,506	16·9	69·3	15·6
Others	10,672	6·0	19,286	5·9	80·7	6·0

TABLE 19
Ethnic Proportions in Industry—Kuala Lumpur, 1947 and 1957
(Figures are percentages)

	Malays		Chinese		Indians		Others	
	1947	1957	1947	1957	1947	1957	1947	1957
Manufacturing	11·8	10·5	73·0	73·1	13·4	15·0	1·5	1·1
Transport and Communications	16·4	23·7	43·7	36·9	33·6	32·1	6·1	7·2
Commerce and Finance	4·9	7·6	75·0	69·4	18·2	20·0	1·7	2·9
Public Administration and Defence	31·7	38·7	22·5	24·4	35·7	19·0	9·9	17·8
Professions and Entertainment	22·8	17·8	54·4	55·6	17·4	21·9	5·5	4·5
Personal Services	10·3	10·4	64·4	69·0	24·2	19·1	0·9	1·6

the city or on its fringes. In addition, their numbers increased in the areas of ethnically-mixed government housing. The occupational structure changed little, however (see Table 19), for the Malays continued to concentrate in those sectors which they had occupied during the colonial period. The immigrant groups continued to dominate the manufacturing and commercial sectors. Politically this was a period of rapid devolution towards independence, which was characterized by the growing Malay ascendancy of political power within the structure of the multi-racial Alliance Party.[21] Despite this increase in national political power and its manipulation from Kuala Lumpur, the Malays still remained a minority, numerically and economically, in the capital city.

The period since Independence[22] superficially has showed

evidence of the most rapid change in the position of the Malay in the city. While there has been no census since 1957, by which to judge the relative increase of the various ethnic groups, a sample survey carried out in 1962–63 of the Kuala Lumpur Malays, indicated only 18 per cent of the household heads interviewed had been born in Kuala Lumpur and some 32 per cent had arrived since the beginning of 1957. Those who had arrived in the period from the beginning of 1947 until the end of 1956 made up 24 per cent and the remaining migrants, 26 per cent. While it is reasonable to assume that there has been some wastage among migrants who have left the city from earlier periods, which has the effect of inflating the proportion of recent migrants, the latter's large proportion still indicates substantial in-movement since 1957.[23]

It is impossible, however, to determine whether this substantial increase in the numbers of Malays in the post-independence period has increased their proportion of the total Kuala Lumpur population. If Caldwell's prediction of the slowing down of Chinese rural–urban migration[24] is accepted, it seems likely that the Malay proportion of the total city population has almost certainly increased. This population increase has led to some changes in the distribution of the Malay community throughout the city, particularly in squatter areas adjacent to the peri-urban legal settlements. Some of the inner-city squatters have been transferred to new housing areas such as Kampong Pandan. Many of the most recent migrants have moved into areas of government housing, but so rapid has been the increase in government employment that there has been a severe shortage of this type of housing (see Figure 14).

One aspect of the ecological location of recent migrant groups frequently commented upon in research on Third World urbanization, has been the tendency for birthplace groups to concentrate in particular parts of the city.[25] Apart from the concentration of Kuala Lumpur-born in the long-established settlement in Kampong Bahru, no such tendencies can be observed in the Kuala Lumpur Malay community (see Figure 15), although historically some of the peri-urban settlements were made up of concentrations of Indonesian immigrants. There is, however, a tendency for occupational

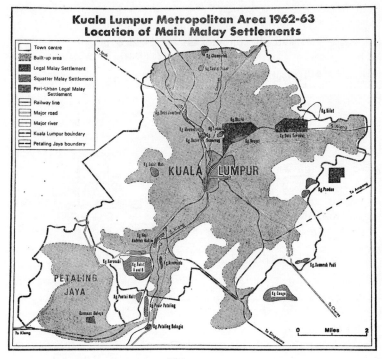

Figure 14

concentration particularly in the areas of government housing (where it is inevitable) and in some of the squatter settlements where proximity to place of employment is an important factor in locating the migrants.[26]

The influence of this in-migration on the age structure of the community is indicated in Figure 16, where the proportion of the various age groups made up of migrants in Kuala Lumpur is contrasted with the age structure of Selangor State. In considering the overall age patterns, the striking fact is the much greater concentration of the Kuala Lumpur population in the working age groups between 15 and 60 years. Within this working age group, migrants dominate except in the youngest age group, 15 to 19 years. In contrast to the age structures of some migrant groups of other Third World cities, there is no pronounced concentration of male migrants in the 15 to 30 age

159

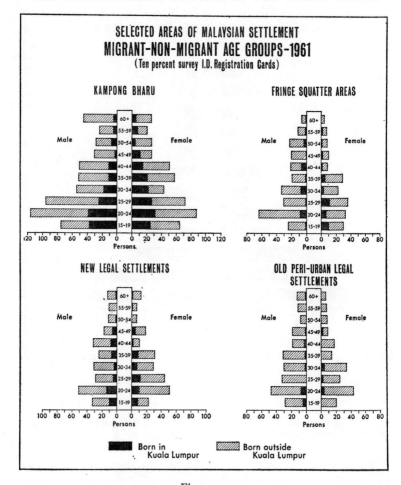

Figure 15

group.[27] The Kuala Lumpur age pyramid shows a surprising concentration of Malay males in their early forties, of which the migrants make a substantial proportion. The overall pattern that emerges is one in which migrants dominate all the working age groups with the exception of the youngest, 15–19 years.

The post-independence period also was characterized by a continuing growth of Malay political power both within the

(A)

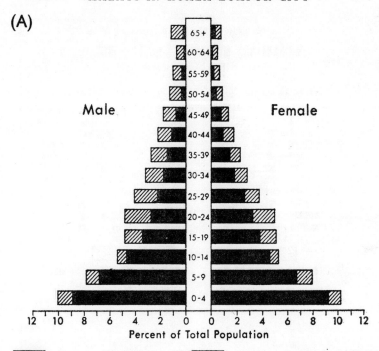

Male | Female

12 10 8 6 4 2 0 0 2 4 6 8 10 12
Percent of Total Population

■ Born in Selangor ▨ Born outside Selangor

Figure 16(A). Migrant and non-migrant Malays, Selangor State, 1957

city and on a wider national scale. For the first time a Malay administrator was appointed to control the new nation's capital. The problem of a Chinese and Indian-dominated City Council was solved by the abolition of elections in the federal capital. The decision to make Malay the national language led to the growth of a number of institutions concerned with promoting the national language, notably the Dewan Bahasa dan Pustaka and the National Language Institute. In addition, new educational institutions were established, notably the University and the Training College. The government push for rural development, social welfare and education all led to a rapid increase in the number of civil servants, many of them Malays. Thus the growth of Kuala Lumpur as the national capital and the increasing political power of the Malays played an important role in the changing position of the community in the city.

(B)

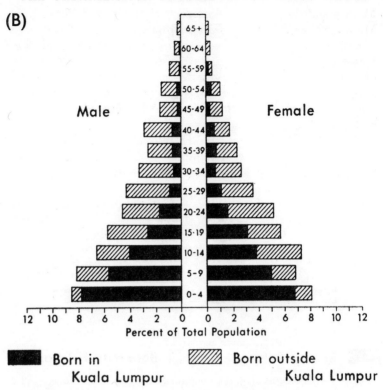

Figure 16(B). Migrant and non-migrant Malays, Kuala Lumpur, 1962–63 Sample

However, while the Malays' political position had changed, their economic position in the city altered little. As Figure 17 indicates, over half the Malay male[28] employees were concentrated in the service sector compared to only a third of the total male-employed population in the Kuala Lumpur Metropolitan area.[29] This heavy concentration simply represented a continuation of the pattern of Malay concentration in the colonial period. While the proportions of Malay males employed in commerce is higher than the 1957 figure (see Table 19), there has been little increase in manufacturing and virtually no employment in the building and construction sector. The striking contrast in the structure of the industrial labour force of

Malays and the total population emphasizes the failure of the Malays to penetrate the most productive sectors of the city's labour force, dominated instead by the immigrant groups. However, the industrial structure of the labour force is of only limited value in measuring this degree of penetration because it takes no account of the status of employment. Thus, for instance a person employed by a bank as a guard on low wages is classified within the commerce category.

The relative position of the Malay males in the city's labour force would be more clearly indicated if data on occupations for the total population were available. Unfortunately there is at present no information on the total city population although the 1962–3 survey did collect occupational data for the Malay community which is shown in Table 20.

TABLE 20

PERCENTAGE OF EMPLOYED MALAY MALES IN OCCUPATIONAL CATEGORIES—
KUALA LUMPUR METROPOLITAN AREA—1962–3 SAMPLE

Occupation	Per cent
Professional	13
Mining	—
Administrative	5
Transport and Communications	16
Clerical	26
Craftsmen	9
Sales and Retail	2
Labourers	11
Agriculture	4
Services and Sport	11
Inadequate classification	3
	100

This table indicates a much wider spread of employment among the Malay males than the heavy concentration revealed in Figure 17. The largest concentration occurs in the clerical occupations where the majority of Malays are employed by the government. Other concentrations occur in professional occupations and transport and communications. Overall the pattern of Malay male employment which emerges from this table seems to contradict that of the industrial employment table for, with the exception of the sales and retail sector, the

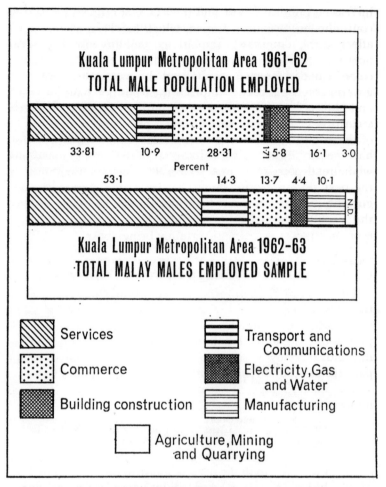

Figure 17. The industrial structure of the total male labour force of Kuala Lumpur Metropolitan Area

Malays appear quite widely spread throughout the various occupational sectors. But the broad divisions of the table mask substantial concentrations within the various occupational categories.

This brief sketch of the history of the Malay community in Kuala Lumpur has emphasized the contrast between their increasing political power and their lack of economic power, a contradiction, it can be argued, which has been a vital factor affecting the patterns of occupational mobility discussed in the next section. Attitudes engendered among the Malays in the colonial period[30] which emphasized the paternalistic role that government could play to improve their position have persisted, and Malays in the city still see their position as one in which the security of government employment is preferable to penetration of the entrepreneurial and commercial sectors for which they have neither the skills nor the capital of the immigrant groups who already dominate these sectors. Occupational mobility, as the next section clearly shows, occurs within a framework of governmental protection which has, for the moment, avoided the problems which the ascendancy to political but not economic power will almost certainly bring about.

OCCUPATIONAL MOBILITY AMONG THE MALAYS

The analysis of the preceding two sections has emphasized the importance of the city's character and the particular socio-economic position and aspirations of the group engaged in the process of occupational mobility. With these two considerations in mind, it is now possible to proceed with the analysis of the patterns of occupational mobility among the Malays.[31]

The method used to measure occupational mobility is as follows:

(i)   In order to test Lipset's hypothesis of cyclical mobility 'in which immigrants or migrants into large cities take over the lower-status positions while the native urban-ites move up in the occupation structure', the household heads have been divided into four main groups by separating the Kuala Lumpur-born from the rest of the migrants and dividing the latter migrant group according to their length of residence in the city: (a) Kuala Lumpur-born; (b) Colonial migrants (those arriving in Kuala Lumpur before the end of 1947); (c) Transitional migrants (those arriving between the beginning of 1947 and the end of 1956); and (d) Post-Independence migrants (those arriving from the beginning of 1957 until the time of the interview in 1963).[32]

(ii) In view of the limitations of the census divisions of occupations as a measure of occupational mobility, an occupational classification was devised which took into account such factors as prestige and income.[33] Occupations were grouped in ten categories and ranked according to status from 0 to 10. The highest occupational category (0) included Cabinet Ministers, High Ranking Service Personnel, Departmental Heads, Members of Parliament, etc. The lowest (10) was made up largely of non-landowning agricultural workers within the peasant sector.[34] In the tables which follow, occupational mobility is measured in three ways: (a) relation of present occupation of household heads to fathers' occupation; (b) relation of last occupation of household head before move to city to present occupation; and (c) relation of first occupation of household head in city to present occupation. In the tables which follow only inter-occupational mobility is measured; i.e., movement from one occupational category to another. Intra-occupational mobility, i.e., the change of occupations within the same occupational category, is not measured.[35] Thus these tables give no indication of job mobility. A change of occupation within the same occupational category is recorded as stable. In the case of upward or downward mobility, this simply records a shift upwards or downwards in the scale between 0 to 10.[36]

The first measure of occupational mobility, the relationship of father's occupation to that of present occupation, is shown in Table 21. It indicates that upward mobility has been the major pattern in the case of the migrant groups although there were sizeable variations between the groups. The higher figure for the transitional migrants is accounted for by the fact that they have the highest proportion of fathers engaged in rural occupations (56 per cent). Contrasted with the general upward mobility of the migrant groups, only half the Kuala Lumpur-born have experienced upward mobility in relation to their fathers' occupation. The substantial proportion who have remained in the same occupational groups or actually experienced downward mobility does not seem to support the assertion

TABLE 21

Direction of Mobility	K-L Born		Post-Ind.		Transitional		Colonial	
	No.	%	No.	%	No.	%	No.	%
Upward	41	51	104	66	88	72	73	59
Stable	22	27	22	14	18	15	25	20
Downward	18	22	32	20	16	13	26	21
TOTAL	81	100	158	100	122	100	124	100
*No Infor.	20		18		12		23	
GRAND TOTAL	101		176		134		147	

* No Information includes those who gave inadequate information on father's occupation and unemployed.

that the urbanite experiences greater occupational mobility than the migrant. It must be admitted, however, that this pattern of inter-generational mobility is partly the result of the classification of occupations which generally downgrades rural occupations. As the urbanite is already further up the scale, it is harder for him to go up the scale. But even so, the supposed advantages of the urbanite—superior knowledge of the city environment and better education—should have given him an advantage which is not evident from this table.

The next measure of occupational mobility allows a much more accurate measure of the assertions of occupational mobility in the city based on Western experience. Table 22 shows the relationship between the last occupation prior to the move to the city to the present occupation of the migrants. Most striking is the sharp contrast in the patterns of occupational mobility between the most recent migrants and those of the earlier period. Almost two-thirds of the post-independence migrants have experienced no inter-occupational mobility in their shift to Kuala Lumpur. There are contrasts, too, between the earlier migrant groupings. Particularly significant is the higher figure of downward mobility in the case of the transitional migrants and the proportion of stable occupations in the case of the colonial migrants. The reasons for this are mixed. In

TABLE 22

MALAY MALE HOUSEHOLD HEADS—KUALA LUMPUR—1962-3 SAMPLE, LAST
OCCUPATION PRIOR TO MOVE TO KUALA LUMPUR TO PRESENT
OCCUPATION

Direction of Mobility	Post Ind. No.	Post Ind. %	Transitional No.	Transitional %	Colonial No.	Colonial %
Upward	45	29	44	47	35	49
Stable	91	59	32	34	31	43
Downward	18	12	18	19	6	8
TOTAL	154	100	94	100	72	100
In School	11		19		45	
No Infor.	11		21		30	
GRAND TOTAL	176		134		147	

the case of the post-independence migrants, the high proportion
of stable occupations is a reflection of the large number of
migrants who have been transferred to the city from government
posts in other parts of the country: 52 per cent of the post-
independence migrants gave transfer as the major reason for
their move compared to 33 per cent and 25 per cent for the
transitional and colonial groups.

The polarization in the transitional migrants between the
groups of upward and downward mobility is explained by
another set of circumstances. The majority of those who had
experienced downward mobility had previously been engaged
in the police, army or special constabulary. The reduction
of the numbers engaged in these sectors, particularly that of the
special constabulary with the defeat of the Communists, forced
many of them on to the labour market and they moved to the
city where many took jobs as drivers, *jagas* and labourers.[37]
Overall the evidence of this table does not indicate that the
move to the city invariably 'provides increased economic
power or confers more prestige'.

Finally the patterns of occupational mobility within the city
can be considered. Here once again it is clear that the patterns
of occupational mobility common in the Western city have
not been repeated. The basic pattern is one of occupational
stability (see Table 23). As would be expected the post-

TABLE 23

MALAY MALE HOUSEHOLD HEADS—KUALA LUMPUR—1962–3 SAMPLE,
FIRST OCCUPATION IN KUALA LUMPUR TO PRESENT OCCUPATION

Direction of Mobility	K-L Born		Post Ind.		Transitional		Colonial	
	No.	%	No.	%	No.	%	No.	%
Upward	21	23	20	12	33	25	40	29
Stable	58	64	141	82	90	68	82	60
Downward	12	13	11	6	10	7	15	11
TOTAL	91	100	172	100	133	100	137	100
No Infor.	10		4		1		10	
GRAND TOTAL	101		176		134		147	

independence migrants who have spent the shortest time in the city have the highest proportion of stability in occupations, but this feature is also affected by the fact that many have been transferred government servants. There is no indication that the native urbanites have shown greater upward mobility than the older migrant groups; indeed, they have the highest proportion of downward occupational mobility. The Kuala Lumpur-born do, however, have the highest proportion of employed who have experienced job mobility—48 per cent of the Kuala Lumpur-born had more than one job in the city, compared to 20 per cent of the post-independence migrants, 35 per cent of the transitional migrants, and 40 per cent of the colonial migrants. This greater job mobility of the Kuala Lumpur-born may well represent a greater awareness of job opportunities and more flexibility in leaving one job for another, but clearly it has not led to great upward mobility. More frequently it involved a change of job within an existing occupational category. One further aspect of the Western pattern of occupational mobility can be investigated at this point. This is the assertion that migrants enter the low-status occupations when they first arrive in the city. As Table 24 indicates, this is certainly not the pattern followed by the Malay migrants. The majority of migrants have entered middle-status occupations in which they have persisted. There is a marked difference in the proportion of migrants entering upper-status occupations, which largely reflects the increasing opportunities accompanying independence.

TABLE 24

MALAY HOUSEHOLD HEADS—KUALA LUMPUR—1962-3 SAMPLE
PERCENTAGE IN OCCUPATIONAL STATUS GROUPS FOR FIRST OCCUPATION IN
KUALA LUMPUR CITY

Status	K-L Born	Post-Ind.	Trans.	Colonial
High	3	17	10	4
Middle	67	53	52	58
Low	30	30	38	38
TOTAL	100 (n=91)	100 (n=172)	100 (n=133)	100 (n=137)

The conclusions that emerge from this analysis are threefold. First, it is clear that the model of occupational mobility based on Western experience is not being experienced in the case of the Kuala Lumpur Malays who have been analysed, since the move to the city does not appear to have greatly improved the occupational status of the Malays. Once within the city, the migrants have remained remarkably stable in their occupations. Nor for that matter have the urban-born experienced greater mobility than the migrants. Secondly, based on the stability of the Malays' occupational position in the city, it may be concluded that the processes favourable to occupational mobility enumerated by Lipset are not all operating. On the other hand, it is not clear from this analysis that the barriers to occupational mobility which are said to exist in the Third World city give an entirely adequate explanation in the Malay case. For instance, employment opportunities appear to have expanded at a fast enough rate in the government and transport sectors to absorb the influx of Malays. But the barriers to occupational mobility posed by the immigrant groups' dominance of the commercial and manufacturing occupations have persisted rather than been removed. The final conclusion, which in effect stems from the first two, emphasizes the uniqueness of the Malay example —the complex intermixture of factors—a capital city inhabited largely by immigrant groups; a ruling party drawing its power from a largely rural base that rules from an urban base; and the fortunate circumstances of independence that allow the ruling ethnic group to slowly ease its population into occupational niches within the city so that they avoid any confrontation with the economically powerful immigrant groups.

CONCLUSION

The implication of this analysis may be treated on two levels. In theoretical terms it emphasizes the need for more empirical studies of occupational mobility in Third World cities before adequate theories can be developed. In practical terms the implications of this study for the future of the Malays in the city may be of some importance. It would appear that in the first five years of independence the Malays were effectively absorbed into the occupational structure of Kuala Lumpur City without greatly disturbing the pattern of ethnic concentration in the various occupational niches which had grown up during the colonial period, but by the end of 1962 certain danger signs were beginning to emerge. A 1962 survey of unemployment reported that rates of unemployment among Malays in the 15–24 age group living in urban areas were very high.[38] It was becoming clear that employment opportunities in Kuala Lumpur city were not expanding at a fast enough rate (despite a considerable growth in industry) to absorb the younger and largely unskilled population which was entering the city. Thus ethnic competition over occupational opportunities which had been avoided amongst the older working groups was beginning to emerge in the younger unemployed groups. What is more, this pattern seems likely to continue for the major part of rural–urban migration will have to be made up of Malays in the future.[39] The danger of such an influx of Malays (not always adequately prepared for urban occupations) into cities where employment opportunities are not enough to absorb the migrant population is obvious. The confrontation between the immigrant group and the indigenous group for the economic power of the city cannot be postponed for long.

Planning to avoid these dangers is not easy. The Malaysian government has placed great emphasis on the possibilities of expanding employment opportunities in the agricultural sector in which it hopes to absorb '70 per cent of the farm youth coming to working age in Malaya',[40] in the period 1966–70. Most of this population will be Malays. Manufacturing is expected to absorb only 10 per cent of the new jobs anticipated, while government and other sectors will absorb the remainder. Thus the government hopes to avoid ethnic competition in the city by allowing a pause during which it can push on with schemes of agricultural development, education, technical training, and the widespread use of Malay as the national language in order to iron out the differences between the ethnic groups inherited from the colonial period.

In practice there seems little alternative to this attempt to hold a balance between the ethnic groups in Malayan society.[41] This policy of gradualism, while it may not always appear economically rational, is certainly socially necessary. Unfortunately, there are a great number of problems associated with this policy. Notable among these problems is the faith placed in the practical realization of the plan's intention to keep such a large proportion of Malays in the agricultural labour force. As Hamzah Sendut has pointed out, while improved conditions in rural areas may lead to fewer people being pushed to the cities, they also involve an increase in productivity which may reduce employment requirements, and they also offer the opportunities of education and improved knowledge of the urban environment which encourage the migrant to move to the city.[42] It is important that the Malaysian government should plan for such eventualities by assuring the Malay the skills which will allow him to enter employment opportunities to become available in the city.[43] At all costs, the situation must be avoided in which the present poverty of the dominantly Malay countryside could be transferred to the city by the mass influx of rural migrants, for under such circumstances a final confrontation between the indigenous and immigrant groups would be inevitable.

NOTES

1. Paul K. Hatt and Albert J. Reiss, Jr. (eds.), *Cities and Society*, 1959, pp. 394–5
2. The literature on this subject is immense. I make no claim to have read more than a small slice of it. The three volumes I found of most use in this study were: Pitirim A. Sorokin's classic pioneer study, *Social Mobility*, 1927, reprinted together with Chapter Five of Vol. IV of *Social and Cultural Dynamics* as *Social and Cultural Mobility*, 1959: Reinhard Bendix and Seymour Martin Lipset (eds.), *Class, Status and Power*, 1954, and David Victor Glass (ed.), *Social Mobility in Britain*, 1954

3. Seymour Martin Lipset, 'Social Mobility and Urbanization', in Hatt and Reiss, op. cit., p. 464

4. Ibid., p. 463

5. See, for instance, John Dollard, *Caste and Class in a Southern Town*, 1949

6. See Andrew W. Lind, *An Island Community: Ecological Succession in Hawaii*, 1938, and *Hawaii's People*, 1955

7. However, a paper by Oscar Lewis does question the basic assumption that occupational mobility is prevalent, let alone desired, by certain groups who live in Western cities. Lewis argues that one of the products of Western capitalism has been to create '. . . a subculture of Western society with its own structure and rationale, a way of life handed on from generation to generation along family lines'. The people who live in this subculture are practitioners of a 'culture of poverty' which 'is both an adaptation and a reaction of the poor to their marginal position in a class-stratified, highly individuated capitalistic society'. This is a group which does not share the values asserted by the dominant class; values that emphasize 'thrift and the accumulation of wealth and property, stresses the possibility of upward mobility and explains low economic status as the results of personal inadequacy and inferiority'. What is more the 'style of life' which characterizes the 'culture of poverty 'transcends national boundaries and regional and rural–urban differences within nations'. The significance of the culture of poverty' to the prospects of occupational mobility in the Third World cities must be clear, for the Third World societies were virtually everywhere moulded and shaped by the penetration of capitalism. Thus in every Third World city substantial numbers of participants in the 'culture of poverty' do not desire or participate in the process of occupational mobility. See Oscar Lewis, 'The Culture of Poverty', *Scientific American*, Vol. 215, No. 4, October, 1966, pp. 19–25

8. For the purposes of this discussion the definition of the Third World accepts the broad delineation of the region put forward by Peter Worsley in *The Third World*, 1964, which excludes the socialist societies of China, Cuba and North Vietnam.

9. This concentration of various ethnic groups within distinct occupational sectors which occurred during the colonial period has been labelled a 'plural society' by J. S. Furnivall in his study *Colonial Policy and Practice*, 1948. The most thorough discussion of the concept occurs in M. G. Smith, *The Plural Society in the British West Indies*, 1965. The problem posed by immigrants' dominance of a large part of the cities' labour forces and the attempts of the indigenous groups to move into these sectors are discussed at some length in my study *The Southeast Asian City: A Social Geography of the Primate Cities of Southeast Asia*, 1967, pp. 85–102

10. Philip M. Hauser (ed.), *Urbanization in Asia and the Far East*, 1957, pp. 87–8

11. One should hasten to add that this situation of economic stagnation with its stultifying effect on occupational mobility does not pertain in every Third World country. But even in countries such as Malaysia and the Philippines, which have experienced some considerable increase

in manufacturing largely concentrated on their capital cities, in the post-independence period, unemployment rates remain high.

12. See Kingsley Davis, 'The Urbanization of the Human Population', *Scientific American*, Vol. 213, No. 3, September, 1965, pp. 41–53

13. See Bert F. Hoselitz, 'The City, The Factory and Economic Growth' in Hatt and Reiss, op. cit., pp. 542–3, for a description of 'central cities'.

14. The history of Kuala Lumpur up to 1890s has been adequately told in J. M. Gullick's *An History of Kuala Lumpur*, 1957, but as yet there is no specific study of the history of the city in the period between 1900 and 1947

15. I have discussed the features of this period in some detail in pp. 121–45. In retrospect I am inclined to think that I overemphasized the static nature of this period of devolution and should have taken more account of the changes that occurred in the period.

16. See Hamzah Sendut, 'The Structure of Kuala Lumpur', *The Town Planning Review*, Vol. 36, No. 2, July, 1965, pp. 125–38, for a thorough discussion of the contemporary functions of Kuala Lumpur.

17. Tregonning has posed this rift between Kuala Lumpur and Singapore as 'a clash between two opposing points of view as typified by a dynamic ocean port and a traditional inland royal capital'. He draws parallels with the clash of values which have occurred in other countries, for instance that between Pretoria and Capetown. While it is possible to argue that he overemphasizes the degree of conservatism in Kuala Lumpur, the concept is a useful one, particularly in view of the increasing tendency for Kuala Lumpur to adopt the symbols of the Malay world rather than those of the Malaysian. See K. G. Tregonning, 'Singapore and Kuala Lumpur: A Politico–Geographical Contrast', *Pacific Viewpoint*, Vol. 7, No. 2, September, 1966, pp. 238–41

18. Throughout this paper the term Malay is defined according to the definition adopted in the Malayan censuses which includes both indigenous and immigrant Malays. In the past the census has grouped these two communities under the joint head of Malaysian, but in view of the creation of the state of Malaysia, and the use of this term to define any citizen of this state, it is clearly inadequate if applied only to Malays.

19. I do not want to deny that the urban centres were centres of Malay nationalism. Indeed there is considerable evidence that they were; see W. R. Roff, 'The Malayo-Muslim World of Singapore at the Close of the Nineteenth Century', *Journal of Asian Studies*, Vol. XXIV, No. 1, November, 1964, pp. 75–90. Also see Mohammad Yunis Hamidi, *Sejarah Pergerakan Politik Melayu Semenanjong*, 1961

20. Perhaps the best example of this attitude was the Malay Agricultural Settlement established in Kuala Lumpur in 1899 by the British Administrators in order to prevent the Malay from becoming corrupted by the urban environment.

21. See T. G. McGee, 'The Malayan Elections of 1959: A Case Study in Electoral Geography', *The Journal of Tropical Geography*, Vol. 16, October, 1962, pp. 70–100

22. This is the period up to the foundation of the State of Malaysia in September 1963. By this time the sample survey of the Malay community which is the source of much of the data used in later sections of the paper had been completed and thus I have not carried on the discussion of the features of the Malay community beyond this date.

23. The 1962–3 sample survey of 560 Malay households in the Kuala Lumpur Metropolitan area covered a total population of 3,238; a 5·3 per cent sample of the estimated Malay population at that time. Difficulties of finance and lack of an adequate sampling frame prevented a random sample being taken, although every effort was made to make the sample as unbiased as possible. Failure to receive permission to interview either police or army personnel probably led to some under-enumeration of males in the 20–29 age group. In addition it seems likely that there was an under-enumeration among Malays engaged in skilled occupations associated with the government-owned railways. Overall, however, comparison with the 1957 census and the 10 per cent random sample of I.D. registration cards indicates no major biases in the sample. Fuller details of the sample are available in T. G. McGee, 'Malays in Kuala Lumpur City: A Geographical Contribution to the Study of Urbanization', unpublished Ph.D.

24. See J. C. Caldwell, 'The Demographic Background', Chapter 3 of T. H. Silcock (ed.), *The Political Economy of Independent Malaya*, 1963, p. 85

25. See, for instance, Janet Abu-Lughod, 'Migrant Adjustment to City Life: The Egyptian Case', *The American Journal of Sociology*, Vol. LXVII, No. 1, July, 1961, pp. 22–32

26. For instance, a squatter kampong such as Kampong Haji Abdullah Hukim, located close to the Lever factory and the major employment centre of the Central Electricity Board had a high proportion of its employed males employed in these two industries.

27. This feature of the demographic structure of the Southeast Asian cities has been discussed in *The Southeast Asian City*. The failure of this pattern to be repeated in the 1962–3 sample is almost certainly due to the exclusion of police and army personnel.

28. Figure 17 shows the proportions of all Malay males in the 1962–3 sample who were employed. The ensuing discussion of Malay labour force characteristics refers only to the male labour force. I have not analysed the pattern of Malay female employment as their participation in the labour force, although increasing, is still very small. Thus of the 786 females in the sample who were in the 15 to 60 age group, only 103 (13 per cent) were employed, compared to 691 (80 per cent) males. The 20 per cent of the males who were not employed consisted of unemployed, those still schooling and those retired from work.

29. The Kuala Lumpur Metropolitan area is shown in Figure 14. It consists of Kuala Lumpur City, as it was defined territorially in 1962, and the dormitory suburb of Petaling Jaya. The 1962–3 survey of Malay households was confined to this area, apart from the inclusion of the squatter kampongs marked on Figure 14 which lay outside city boundaries.

30. I realize that I am treading on thin ice in venturing into the question of the attitudes engendered by colonialism. I have been struck by the similarity of the arguments, despite a wide variation in ideological positions, and relevance to the Malayan experience of four major studies of this question. All stress the paternalistic relationship which grew up between colonial ruler and those ruled. All stress, with varying degrees of intensity, that the major result of this colonial impact was to create a Westernized and urban middle class who have become the heirs of colonial rule. All stress the static social impact of the colonial rule which had the effect in many cases of freezing social institutions and relationships which were in a state of flux. In the case of Malaya, the effect of the colonial impact was to concentrate the Malays in the peasant sector; the immigrant groups, in the estate, mining and urban sectors; and to build up attitudes in the Westernized upper middle class which accepted this pattern as something reflecting the relative skills and desires of the main ethnic groups. While I know it is a controversial position, I am convinced that such attitudes still persist among the contemporary elites of Malaya, and this is one reason for the continued emphasis in economic planning to keep the Malay in agricultural occupations. The four studies referred to earlier in the note are: O. Mannoni, *Prospero and Caliban: The Psychology of Colonialism*, 1956; Everett E. Hagen, *On the Theory of Social Change*, 1962; Frantz Fanon, *The Damned*, 1963; and Nirad C. Chaudhuri, *The Continent of Circe*, 1965

31. The analysis which follows is based only on data for household heads. Information on the entire Malay male labour force was not sufficient to allow a detailed analysis of their patterns of occupational mobility. The fact that this data on occupational mobility is available only for household heads imposes certain limitations on the analysis. First, because the survey used houses as the basic sampling unit, and households as the interviewing units and excluded other forms of institutional housing, the nuclear family was by far the most prominent household unit. Such household units were generally well established and the household heads often employed in established occupations. The survey does not include younger members of the household whose patterns of occupational mobility may have shown substantial variations from those of the household heads. Another fact to consider is the reliability of the data on prior occupations; respondents often tend to exaggerate the importance of earlier occupations. Every effort was made to check on the reliability of this information both by cross-checks within the questionnaire and by personal interviews in some cases. If there was any doubt, the data has not been incorporated in these tables.

32. Some argument might be voiced with respect to the choice of these time divisions for the migrants. Strictly the nomenclature, post-independence migrants, should only apply to those migrants who arrived after August, 1957, but the movement to independence was so rapid in this year that the migrants represented the preliminary movement of the post-independence migrants. The divisions reflect the main periods of socio-political evolution in the Malay community as well as the length of residence in the city. It must be also emphasized that these groups represent pure abstractions; apart from rather closer kinship ties amongst the Kuala Lumpur-born, I could find no recognition of group-

ings according to length of residence in the city by the Malay community. One further aspect of the groupings needs to be clarified. This is the role that the differentials of age and education between these groups played in affecting the mobility of the groups. Of the four age groups the colonial migrants have the highest median age of 43 years; the Kuala Lumpur-born, a median age of 36 years; the transitional migrants 35 years and the post-independence, 33 years. Thus the colonial migrants have the greatest opportunity of upward mobility as they have been in the labour force the longest period. There is very little difference between the other groups in this respect. The possibilities of occupational mobility are also affected by the educational background of the various groupings. Here there is little difference between the groups. All have approximately half of their group with Malay primary education only, although there is a higher proportion of English secondary-educated and higher educated groups in the Kuala Lumpur-born and post-Independence groupings which certainly accounts for their higher proportion in the upper status occupations.

33. In the absence of any study of occupational prestige, the classification of occupations did involve certain arbitrary decisions on my part as to the scaling of various occupations. S. Husin Ali's important study of social stratification in Malay rural society does provide some information on rural stratification. See *Social Stratification in Kampong Bagan*, 1964, Monograph of the Malaysian Branch Royal Asiatic Society, University of Malaya. As yet, unfortunately, there has been no comparable study of Malay urban stratification. Michael Swift suggests some broad social groupings in his study, *Malay Peasant Society in Jelebu*, 1965. In the main I have relied on data from answers to a question in the survey on occupations desired for children as an indicator of occupational prestige, and followed the broad framework of a classification of occupations adopted in a survey of Petaling Jaya. See T. G. McGee and W. D. McTaggart, *Petaling Jaya: A Socio-Economic Survey of a New Town in Selangor, Malaysia*, Pacific Viewpoint Monograph, No. 2, 1967, pp. 46–7

34. See Appendix for the classification adopted.

35. Sorokin, op. cit., discusses this distinction between inter- and intra-occupational mobility at some length in his study of social mobility. See pp. 99–130

36. This technique is used in C. Wright Mills et. al., *The Puerto Rican Journey*, 1950, pp. 60–76

37. The significant expansion in numbers of the police, army and special forces which was associated with the Emergency and substantial recruitment of Malays from rural areas into these occupations played a major role in dislocating the Malay from the rural sector. No event, apart from Independence, has opened the channels of vertical circulation for the Malay to such an extent.

38. See Department of Labour and Industrial Relations and Department of Statistics, *Report on Employment, Unemployment and Underemployment, 1963*, which recorded that unemployment was highest in the large cities (over 100,000) and particularly high in the age group 15–24

39. See Caldwell's estimates on the likely component of rural–urban migration that will be made up of Malays, op. cit., p. 85. Hamzah Sendut suggests that the decline in urban fertility amongst the Chinese and high birth rates among the urban Malays will also account for a substantial increase in the numerical proportion of Malays in the cities. See Hamzah Sendut, 'Contemporary Urbanization in Malaysia', *Asian Survey*, Vol. VI, No. 9, September, 1966, pp. 484–91

40. *First Malaysia Plan, 1966–1970*, 1965, p. 80

41. By 'balance' I do not mean to suggest that the social positions of the main ethnic groups would remain the same but, rather, that the balance of political and economic power would remain much the same until the social and economic measures necessary to produce a unified society have begun to produce results.

42. Hamzah Sendut, op. cit., pp. 489–90

43. It is significant that the high rates of unemployment among the 15–19 age group in urban areas is already a major concern of the planners and that 'consideration is now being given to the possibility of establishing a National Youth Pioneer Corps in which unemployed youths will be given productive work along with practical training and experience designed to make them better equipped for employment', *First Malaysia Plan, 1966–1970*, p. 82

APPENDIX

Occupational Classification adopted for study of Malay Occupational Mobility in Kuala Lumpur

UPPER STATUS

0—Elite: Cabinet Ministers; Members of Federal Parliament; High Ranking Service Personnel (General rank or above); Department Heads; Supreme Court Judges; Sultans; University Professors; Physicians.

1—Managerial, Administrative and Professional—Upper Status: Members of State Legislature; Dentists, Lawyers, Bank Managers; Division I Civil Service; Businessmen with incomes above 25,000 Malayan dollars per annum; University Lecturers; Accountants; Architects.

2—Managerial, Administrative and Professional—Lower Status: Secondary School Teachers; Religious officials; e.g. Imam, Kathi; Artists; Writers; Journalists; Businessmen with incomes of between 6,000 and 25,000 Malayan dollars per annum; Police Superintendents; Officers in Services.

MIDDLE STATUS

3—High Clerical, etc.: Chief Clerks; Penghulus; Draughtsmen; Hospital Attendants; Laboratory Assistants; Proprietors with incomes of between 3,000 and 6,000 Malayan dollars; Midwives; Nurses; Religious Teachers; Trained Teachers in primary schools; Police Inspectors; Salesmen in large businesses.

4—Skilled Workers, etc.: Carpenters, Plumbers; Electricians, Mechanics; Compositors, Technicians; Linesmen; Agricultural Supervisors; Mining Assistants; Proprietors with incomes of between 1,000 and 3,000 Malayan dollars.

5—Clerical Workers—Lower Grades; Teachers (unqualified); Police

Constables; and Service Personnel below Sergeant; Peons, Small shop proprietors with incomes below 1,000 Malayan dollars; Ketua Kampongs; Bomohs; Salesmen in small businesses.

LOW STATUS

6—Drivers, etc.: Liftmen; Locomotive drivers; Bus drivers; Taxi drivers; Storemen; Sailors; Hawkers.

7—Factory workers, etc.: Janitors; Domestic servants; Greasers, etc.; Gardeners.

8—Small farmers owning land below 10 acres; Fishermen; Estate workers.

9—Urban labourers employed on daily basis.

10—Non-landowning agricultural worker in peasant sector.